D0386964

Presented to:

_____

Presented by:

_____

Date:

_____

GOD'S
ROAD MAP
FOR WOMEN

Bordon and Winters

WARNER
Faith®

New York Boston Nashville

God's Road Map for Women
Copyright © 2006 Bordon-Winters LLC

All rights reserved. No part of this book may be reproduced in any form or by any electronic or mechanical means, including information storage and retrieval systems, without permission in writing from the publisher, except by a reviewer who may quote brief passages in a review.

Project developed by Bordon Books, Tulsa, Oklahoma
Concept: Bordon and Winters
Project Writing and Compilation: Vicki J. Kuyper and Betsy Williams in association with SnapdragonGroupSM Editorial Services.

Warner Faith
1271 Avenue of the Americas, New York, NY 10020
Visit our Web site at www.warnerfaith.com

The Warner Faith name and logo are registered trademarks of the Time Warner Book Group.

Printed in the United States of America
First Edition: September 2006
10 9 8 7 6 5 4 3 2 1

ISBN: 0-446-57890-8

LCCN: 2006921573

INTRODUCTION

The road of life, as you know if you've been walking on it for very long, has many unmarked intersections and cross streets. Not only that, but it weaves up, down, and around through all types of landscapes and terrains. The journey provides moments of breathtaking beauty and others of abject fear. There are dark stretches, detours, and of course, there is the danger of getting lost. What's a traveler to do? Happily, God has provided a road map—the Bible—to help us avoid dangerous and time-consuming delays and keep us on the path to our desired destination.

In *God's Road Map for Women*, we have mined the Bible for wisdom and understanding that will be especially helpful for those who, like you, are dealing with the issues and challenges common to the fairer sex. We've included Scriptures on certain topics of particular interest to women and laid them out in an A-Z format so they will be simple for you to find and follow. We've also added to each topic an illustrative Bible story or practical devotional to help you on your way. Finally, we've provided heartfelt prayers and letters that express some of the thoughts and feelings God has given in His Word.

We hope you will find all you need as you travel the road of life and reach your next destination safely.

The Publishers

CONTENTS

Aging 10
   Become a Wabi-Sabi Woman 11
Beauty 12
   Boundless Beauty 13
Celebration 14
   Lifestyle of the Blessed and Famous 16
Challenges 18
   From Mourning to Dancing 19
Change 20
   Harvesttime 21
Character 22
   Who Are You? 24
Church 26
   All Pumped Up 27
Commitment 28
   Weathering the Storm 29
Communication 30
   Lost in Translation 32
Compassion 34
   The Great Shoe Exchange 35
Confidence 36
   Assured and Secure 37
Contentment 38
   Heart Hunger 40
Courage 42
   Risking It All 43
Daily Walk 44
   The Journey of a Lifetime 45
Doubt 46
   Unfocused View 48
Emotions 50
   Emotional Balance 51
Encouragement 52
   On the Road Again 53
Eternal Life 54
   Life Quest 56
Expectations 58
   Great Expectations 59
Faith 60

One Act of Faith 61
Faithfulness 62
A Relationally Healthy Habit 64
Fear 66
Fear Factors 67
Forgiveness 68
The First Stone 69
Freedom 70
Born to Be Wild 72
Friendship 74
Hand in Hand, Heart-to-Heart 75
Generosity 76
Two-Coin Treasure 77
Gentleness 78
Gentle Strength 80
God's Faithfulness 82
Trustworthy and True 83
God's Love 84
Once upon Eternity 85
God's Presence 86
Forever by Your Side 88
God's Will 90
The Treasure Inside 91
God's Word 92
The Well-Traveled Woman 93
Grace 94
Erased for Eternity 96
Grief 98
At the Crossroads 99
Guidance 100
Staying in Step with God 101
Guilt 102
Preventing False Alarms 104
Health 106
The Healing Touch 107
Holy Spirit 108
Signs of Life 109
Hope 110
Hope Floats 112
Humility 114
An Accurate Image 115

Identity 116
The Real You 117
Integrity 118
Virtuous or Virtual? 120
Jesus Christ 122
Relationship Paints a Picture 123
Joy 124
Are You in Your Skin? 125
Love 126
Love in Action 128
Ministry 130
Your Impact on the World 131
Nurturing 132
Nurturers Need Nurturing Too 133
Obedience 134
Choose Your Shoes Wisely 136
The Opposite Sex 138
The Balance of the Sexes .139
Patience 140
Watching and Waiting 141
Peace 142
The Path to Peace 144
Perseverance 146
Don't Give Up 147
Power 148
Just Plug In 149
Prayer 150
Portrait of Prayer 152
Priorities 154
The Law of Love 155
Purity 156
It All Comes Out in the Wash 157
Purpose 158
Purpose by Design 160
Quietness and Solitude 162
Stitched Together with Serenity 163
Redemption 164
Ransomed by Love 165
Rejection 166
Never an Outsider 168
Relationships 170

Getting Up Close and Personal 171
Renewal 172
A Brand-New Chapter 173
Repentance 174
The Road to Repentance 176
Restoration 178
Untold Riches 179
Resurrection 180
Risen 181
Righteousness 182
What Would Jesus Do? 184
Sacrifice 186
You're Deeply Loved 187
Seeking God 188
Looking for Love in All the Right Places 189
Sincerity 190
A Gift from the Heart 192
Spiritual Growth 194
How Does Your Garden Grow? 195
Strength 196
Strength for Every Battle 197
Thankfulness 198
The Gift of Gratitude 200
Thoughts 202
Change Your Mind 203
Time 204
Know Your Limits 205
Trials 206
Unexpected Journey 208
Truth 210
One Hundred Percent Genuine 211
Vision 212
Beyond Circumstance 213
Wisdom 214
Wise Words 216
Work 218
On the Job 219
Worship 220
A Lifestyle of Praise 221
Topical Index 222

Aging

The beauty of the aged is their gray hair.
PROVERBS 20:29 NRSV

Is not wisdom found among the aged?
Does not long life bring understanding?
JOB 12:12

Gray hair is like a crown of honor;
it is earned by living a good life.
PROVERBS 16:31 NCV

The older women . . . should be teachers of goodness.
These older women must train the younger women . . .
so that the Christian faith can't be spoken against
by those who know them.
TITUS 2:3-5 TLB

Even to your old age and gray hairs
I am he, I am he who will sustain you.
I have made you and I will carry you;
I will sustain you and I will rescue you.
ISAIAH 46:4

BECOME A WABI-SABI WOMAN

Picture the exquisite patina of an old iron gate, one that's weathered the storms of life. Consider a leather-bound book that has been well loved and well used, its binding a bit broken and pages dog-eared, yet invitingly beautiful in its imperfection. Bring to mind a piece of sea glass, its once jagged edges worn smooth by the pounding of the ocean surf. Each of these items illustrates a Japanese concept of artistic beauty called wabi-sabi.

This wabi-sabi kind of beauty is found in common items whose appearance has been transformed over time—items that are perishable, imperfect, and even incomplete. Its charm is found in a humble and unpretentious appearance. What better way to face your future than as a wabi-sabi woman?

A woman who is well worn and well loved because she's living a full life is intrinsically beautiful. She has a patina of wisdom and experience that rounds her edges and softens her heart. The more you learn to see yourself and others through wabi-sabi eyes, the more you'll see people the way your heavenly Father does.

Take a fresh look in the mirror. Ask God to help you see your own wabi-sabi. Refuse to compare your appearance with those of other women—especially those younger than you. Choose to celebrate the season of life you're in—from spring straight through to winter. Look for the unique beauty each new season brings out in you. Let your wabi-sabi shine through from the inside out.

Beauty

Don't be concerned about the outward beauty that depends
on jewelry, or beautiful clothes, or hair arrangement.
Be beautiful inside, in your hearts, with the lasting charm of a
gentle and quiet spirit which is so precious to God. That kind
of deep beauty was seen in the saintly women of old, who
trusted God and fitted in with their husbands' plans.

1 PETER 3:3-5 TLB

Charm is deceptive, and beauty is fleeting;
but a woman who fears the LORD is to be praised.

PROVERBS 31:30

The Lord said, "God sees not as man sees,
for man looks at the outward appearance,
but the LORD looks at the heart."

1 SAMUEL 16:7 NASB

The LORD taketh pleasure in his people:
he will beautify the meek with salvation.

PSALM 149:4 KJV

How beautiful on the mountains are the feet of those
who bring good news of peace and salvation, the news that
the God of Israel reigns!

ISAIAH 52:7 NLT

BOUNDLESS BEAUTY

One of God's many names written in Scripture is "the Rose of Sharon." You've been created in the image of this eternal Rose. Like a rose, you are intrinsically beautiful. Your beauty goes far beyond what the world would have you believe and far deeper than what you see in the mirror. It can't be measured by the form of your face or the weight you read on the scale. Your beauty is evident in every cell of your body and stir of your spirit. The more you follow in the footsteps of your heavenly Father, the more you grow to resemble Him—and the more beautiful you become.

That's why the most effective beauty treatments are those that work from the inside out. Instead of the mirror, check your heart for blemishes. Ask God to reveal any weaknesses you need to confront, any bad choices you need to confess, or any past hurts you need to forgive. But also ask God to help you see yourself the way He does—as a husband sees His beloved bride standing at the altar: dazzling, radiant, pure, alluring, desirable, beautiful in every sense of the word.

Get in the habit of seeing yourself through God's eyes instead of comparing yourself to the images you see in magazines or on TV. Never before in the history of the world—and never again throughout the length of eternity—will God create another woman with your unique beauty. God revels in who you are, both inside and out. Why not join Him right here, right now?

Celebration

Encourage each other and build each other up,
just as you are already doing.
1 THESSALONIANS 5:11 NLT

The father of the prodigal son said,
"Let's have a feast and celebrate.
For this son of mine was dead and is alive again;
he was lost and is found."
So they began to celebrate.
LUKE 15:23-24

One generation will commend your works to another;
they will tell of your mighty acts.
. . . They will celebrate your abundant goodness
and joyfully sing of your righteousness.
PSALM 145:4,7

The LORD your God in your midst,
The Mighty One, will save;
He will rejoice over you with gladness,
He will quiet you with His love,
He will rejoice over you with singing.
ZEPHANIAH 3:17 NKJV

Heavenly Father,

My heart is so full today that I'm about to explode. There are so many reasons to celebrate that I can hardly keep count!

First, I celebrate You and my life in You. Everything I have and everything I am is because of You and Your abundant goodness in my life. I celebrate Jesus and His triumph over the devil, sin, and every evil thing. I celebrate with all the angels of heaven because of the glorious victory He won through the resurrection.

I also have cause to celebrate the wonderful blessing that others have been to me. Give me opportunities to express my appreciation for each one, and give me words of encouragement to celebrate all the good things You are doing in their lives.

Every day is a day of celebration in You, Lord. I rejoice and give You praise.

Amen.

LIFESTYLE OF THE BLESSED AND FAMOUS

Celebration is an important part of life. Whether it's Christmas Eve, a birthday, a promotion, an anniversary, losing ten pounds, or making a new friend—reasons for you to celebrate abound.

But what does it really mean to celebrate something or someone? The dictionary says that to celebrate means to praise something publicly or make it famous.[1] That's where celebrities get their title. What and whom you celebrate says a lot about who you are. Regarding all those you love as true celebrities—ones who are worthy of praise—means that you have cause for celebration every day. But having cause to celebrate and actually celebrating are two different things.

Consider how you can better celebrate what's important to you. Begin by identifying the true celebrities in your life. They may include your family and friends, your personal heroes, and your faithful heavenly Father. Go beyond what's traditional. Praise them publicly and privately in spontaneous and creative ways. Send a balloon bouquet to a friend at work. Take your mom or dad to lunch as an expression of your appreciation. Take a morning to go for a walk and just sing songs of thanks and praise to God. How, whom, and what you celebrate will be as unique as you are.

Along the way, remember to take time to celebrate you. God does. The Bible says that He sings and rejoices over you. He's making you "famous" in ways that count by helping your authentic, beautiful self shine into the lives of others as you mature into the woman He designed you to be.

My Precious Child,

Oh, how it thrills My heart to hear your words of praise and thanksgiving! Truly each day is a day of celebration, for I am always good and desire to shower you with blessings.

Did you know that I celebrate you? From the day you were conceived, I have rejoiced in the precious person you are. Unlike any other, you are one of My jewels. Your very being makes Me smile.

It grieves my heart when sadness and discouragement begin to cloud your mind. They dampen your spirit and cut off the flow of joy. Know that regardless of any circumstance you face, you have cause for celebration. Lift your eyes, see things from My perspective, and embrace My Word. These things will boost your spirits once again, and you will see that I am causing everything to work for your good and My glory.

Your loving Father

Challenges

Consider it a sheer gift, friends, when tests and challenges come at you from all sides. You know that under pressure, your faith-life is forced into the open and shows its true colors. So don't try to get out of anything prematurely. Let it do its work so you become mature and well-developed, not deficient in any way.

JAMES 1:2-4 MSG

Jesus said, "I've told you all this so that trusting me, you will be unshakable and assured, deeply at peace. In this godless world you will continue to experience difficulties. But take heart! I've conquered the world."

JOHN 16:33 MSG

You, dear children, are from God and have overcome them, because the one who is in you is greater than the one who is in the world.

1 JOHN 4:4

Despite all these things, overwhelming victory is ours through Christ, who loved us.

ROMANS 8:37 NLT

I can do everything with the help of Christ who gives me the strength I need.

PHILIPPIANS 4:13 NLT

FROM MOURNING TO DANCING

Katherine Luther dons her solitary black dress—the one she reserves for times of mourning. Although a young woman, Katherine has already endured many challenges. Her parents place her in a convent at the age of nine. At the age of sixteen, she becomes a nun. Seven years later, stirred by the words of Martin Luther, she decides to leave the Catholic church. Risking severe punishment, Katherine slips out of the convent hidden in a barrel labeled "herring."

At the age of twenty-five, Katherine marries a man seventeen years her senior—the same man whose words once stirred her heart to pursue a new path toward God. Martin and Katherine Luther have six children together, two of whom die young. Today, once again, Katherine dresses herself in the color of grief in time to meet her husband as he returns home for the night. His demeanor is the same as it has been for weeks: his posture stooped, his eyes downcast, his mood solemn and despondent. Katherine's evening attire startles him.

"Who died?" he asks apprehensively.

"God," retorts Katherine.

"You foolish woman," Martin says, "what are you talking about?"

Katherine replies matter-of-factly, "It must be true or else my husband would not be so filled with sorrow." Her ploy works. Martin's mood and attitude change for the better almost immediately.[2]

Everyone faces challenges—even people whose famous faith seems unshakeable. But God is alive and well. He has a plan—and the power—to see you through. Change out of your mourning clothes and into your dancing shoes. With God, every challenge is an opportunity in disguise.

Change

The Lord says,
"Do not remember the former things,
Nor consider the things of old.
Behold, I will do a new thing,
Now it shall spring forth;
Shall you not know it?
I will even make a road in the wilderness
And rivers in the desert."

ISAIAH 43:18·19 NKJV

Moses said, "The LORD himself will go before you.
He will be with you; he will not leave or forget you.
Don't be afraid and don't worry."

DEUTERONOMY 31:8 NCV

God said,
"I'll go ahead of you,
clearing and paving the road."

ISAIAH 45:2 MSG

I am the LORD, I change not.

MALACHI 3:6 KJV

HARVESTTIME

When the sharp winds of winter grow milder, the days grow longer, and the ground is once again covered with the downy green of springtime, apple blossoms begin to bud. As days pass, the buds mature and open, giving off a short-lived perfume that invites insects to pollinate every bloom. But it is only when the flower dies and falls away that the true purpose of an apple tree can be fulfilled. Only then can it begin to bear fruit.

Change is a natural part of God's world. But what is natural isn't always comfortable. When an apple blossom withers and dies, something beautiful disappears. That doesn't mean there won't be beauty and purpose in the days ahead. It simply means change is afoot. In the same way, leaving the beauty of what you've known to grab hold of what lies ahead can often feel more like a rending of your heart than an adventure of the soul. But don't let your emotions or fear of the unknown keep you stuck in one place. Anticipate the journey of traveling down a brand-new road—one that leads you closer to God's greater purpose for your life.

Companies downsize. Friends move. Wrinkles happen. But anytime you're faced with a change in life, you're also faced with new opportunities. Celebrate the beauty of the passing season. Then, turn to God for the courage you need to move ahead. It may be the perfect time for you to harvest a bumper crop of brand-new, beautiful memories.

Character

The character of even a child can be known by the way he acts—
whether what he does is pure and right.

PROVERBS 20:11 TLB

We also exult in our tribulations,
knowing that tribulation brings about perseverance;
and perseverance, proven character;
and proven character, hope.

ROMANS 5:3-4 NASB

A wife of noble character who can find?
She is worth far more than rubies.

PROVERBS 31:10

Do not be misled: "Bad company corrupts good character."

1 CORINTHIANS 15:33

A wife of noble character is her husband's crown.

PROVERBS 12:4

Until the time came to fulfill his word,
the LORD tested Joseph's character.

PSALM 105:19 NLT

Heavenly Father,

Doesn't anyone care about character issues anymore? People commonly cheat on their taxes, are unfaithful to their spouses, break contracts, default on loans, keep the overage when a clerk undercharges, use cable without paying for it—the list is endless. On the other hand, it seems rare to find those who strive for excellence in their character.

I want to be one of the rare ones, Father. Even when I'm stressed-out and overwhelmed, help me to put others first, to be considerate and kind, to be a person of my word. Your character is flawless, and I want the same to be said of me. Help me learn to yield to the fruit of Your Spirit in every situation so that I represent You well.

Amen.

WHO ARE YOU?

Throughout the Bible, God is often described in masculine terms to portray a sense of His power and strength. He is a Warrior, a Father, a Judge, a King, and a Groom waiting for His beloved bride. But God is God—not man. Even though traditionally God is referred to as "He," God is beyond gender—and, if the truth be told, far beyond any accurate description using mere human words. That's why Scripture also describes God by more general metaphors such as "a strong tower," "a cleft in the rock," "the balm of Gilead," "the Rose of Sharon," or "a pillar of fire." God carries us in His arms, shields us with His shadow, and hides us beneath His wings. He is Living Water, the Light of the World, and the Bread of Life. He's the Alpha and the Omega—the Beginning and the End.

In Jewish culture, a name was more than just something parents used to call a child to dinner. A name was chosen to fit a person's character. That's why in Scripture God often changed people's names after they had a life-altering encounter with Him.

The book of Revelation says God has a name for you that you don't yet know—one that accurately describes who you really are. The closer you get to God, the closer you are to becoming the person God created you to be—to living up to your true name. If God whispered your true name to you today, what do you think that name would be?

My Precious Child,

What you are seeing is a sign of the times, and things will get worse. I said in My Word that in the last days people would be lovers of themselves. Worldly people consider truth to be a relative concept and don't think twice about telling "little white lies." They don't see anything wrong with breaking the rules and living only for themselves, for their minds have become clouded due to the darkness that fills the earth.

This, of course, goes against My way of doing things, but it is a tremendous opportunity for you to let your light shine. When My people choose to allow Me to live through them—to be people with spotless character—others will see aspects of My nature and be drawn to My goodness. So let your light shine. Be a person of sterling character. Be a Christ person.

Your loving Father

Church

Christ is the head of the church, his body, of which he is the
Savior. . . . We are members of his body.
EPHESIANS 5:23, 30

Let us not give up meeting together, as some are in the habit
of doing, but let us encourage one another—and all the more
as you see the Day approaching.
HEBREWS 10:25

Jesus said, "Where two or three have gathered together in My
name, I am there in their midst."
MATTHEW 18:20 NASB

All of you together are the one body of Christ and each one of
you is a separate and necessary part of it.
1 CORINTHIANS 12:27 TLB

Each one should use whatever gift he has received to serve
others, faithfully administering God's grace in its various
forms. If anyone speaks, he should do it as one speaking the
very words of God. If anyone serves, he should do it with the
strength God provides, so that in all things God may be
praised through Jesus Christ.
1 PETER 4:10-11

ALL PUMPED UP

Churches are the service stations along the road of life. You can drive around for a while on your own—working, parenting, planning—but eventually, you're going to run low on spiritual fuel. Praying and studying the Bible on your own are essential, but these aren't enough to fill your inner tank to overflowing.

You need to connect with others who are on the same journey you are. People who will help answer questions you may have about the Bible. People who will hold you accountable to apply what you know. People who will serve you and whom you can serve in return. People who will comfort you, inspire you, challenge you, make you laugh, and yes, sometimes even drive you a little nuts. People who will teach you what community and unconditional love are all about.

Churches vary as much as service stations. Some have been around for years and boast a single pump and restroom. Others are super sleek with room for thirty cars to fill up at the same time—not to mention a salad and cappuccino bar. The choice of premium or regular is totally up to you. As long as a church is firmly planted along the Jesus Road that leads straight to heaven, it is worth considering. Choose to become involved with the one that fits you and your personal journey best.

Then, at least once a week, pull on in. Serve and be served. You'll find yourself spiritually pumped and ready to face the week ahead.

Commitment

If you love someone you will be loyal to him
no matter what the cost.

1 CORINTHIANS 13:7 TLB

What happens when we live God's way? He brings gifts into
our lives, much the same way that fruit appears in an
orchard—things like affection for others, exuberance about
life, serenity. We develop a willingness to stick with things, a
sense of compassion in the heart, and a conviction that a basic
holiness permeates things and people. We find ourselves
involved in loyal commitments, not needing to force our way
in life, able to marshal and direct our energies wisely.

GALATIANS 5:22-23 MSG

We'll stick to our assigned tasks of prayer and
speaking God's Word.

ACTS 6:4 MSG

Each person must be responsible for himself.

GALATIANS 6:5 NCV

Many will say they are loyal friends,
but who can find one who is really faithful?

PROVERBS 20:6 NLT

WEATHERING THE STORM

The raindrops pick up speed and size. They pound on Laurel's umbrella like a marching band's percussion section. The rhythmic beat inspires Laurel to pick up the pace of her journey. She quickly makes her way to each front door on the block, looping the rubber band that holds the plastic-bag-protected paper around every doorknob.

"Please come to our garage sale this Saturday!" read the bright blue letters on the printed flyer. "All proceeds go the Red Cross to help victims of Hurricane Katrina."

At thirteen, Laurel and her friends don't have much money of their own. But one thing they agree on: they do have a lot of stuff. That's how the idea of using their stuff to help others who had lost their stuff started. The idea turned into a plan—and a plan into flyers. And that's how Laurel ends up walking around her block on a wet Tuesday afternoon. She didn't know it would be this cold and uncomfortable when she said she'd do this job—but the weather doesn't matter. She'll get the chance to dry off at home soon enough. What matters is her promise and reaching the goal she sees beyond the storm.

Becoming an employee, becoming a wife, becoming a mother, becoming a volunteer, becoming a woman who chooses to follow God—any commitment you make includes an intrinsic promise that you'll actually do what you've said you'll do. Regardless of the weather, your emotions, or circumstances that may make your commitment more difficult to fulfill than you expect, keep your promises. With God's help, there's no storm you cannot weather to be a woman who's faithful and true.

Communication

The right word at the right time
is like a custom-made piece of jewelry.
PROVERBS 25:11 MSG

A gentle response defuses anger,
but a sharp tongue kindles a temper-fire.
PROVERBS 15:1 MSG

Let your conversation be always full of grace,
seasoned with salt, so that you may know
how to answer everyone.
COLOSSIANS 4:6

Let no evil talk come out of your mouths,
but only what is useful for building up,
as there is need, so that your words may
give grace to those who hear.
EPHESIANS 4:29 NRSV

Gracious speech is like clover honey—
good taste to the soul, quick energy for the body.
PROVERBS 16:24 MSG

Heavenly Father,

I've heard it said that communication is the lifeblood of any relationship. The problem is, many times it's downright difficult—especially when dealing with conflicts. In the heat of the battle, it is so easy to let words fly that can injure others and make matters worse. I know I've said things I didn't really mean, but sadly, I can never take those words back.

Help me, Lord, to articulate the things that are in my heart so that they are easy to understand and receive. And help me to hear clearly what others say to me. When I misunderstand, prompt me to seek more information.

Last, I want to be skilled at communicating the Good News so You can use me to draw others to You. You are the ultimate Communicator, Father, and I look to You to help me develop in this area.

Amen.

LOST IN TRANSLATION

Communicating clearly with others isn't always easy, especially if the words you're trying to use are not part of your mother tongue.

A hotel flyer in Shanghai announces: "Special Room Rats in August."

A sign in a Bucharest hotel lobby informs: "The lift is being fixed for the next day. During that time we regret that you will be unbearable."

A notice posted near a hotel swimming pool in France warns: "Swimming is forbidden in the absence of a savior."[3]

But the truth is, you don't have to try speaking another language to wind up being misunderstood. It happens every day. You tell a coworker you hope to be finished with a project by the end of the day, but he interprets your words to mean, "I promise it will be finished." You tell a friend you've got to hang up because it's time for dinner, but what she hears is you don't really care about her or her problems.

While you're not responsible for how others interpret what you say, God does hold you accountable for every word that comes out of your mouth—so choose each one carefully. One way to do that is to pay attention when others speak. Really listen instead of rehearsing in your mind what you want to say. Ask questions when something is unclear. This can stop a misunderstanding before it starts.

When you do open your mouth, consider every word a gift. The book of Proverbs compares carefully chosen words to the masterfully crafted beauty of a piece of gold jewelry. Select only the very best, words that are appropriate and beneficial to those listening—which includes God himself. Make everything you say pure twenty-four karat gold.

My Precious Child,

Some are naturally better communicators than others, but everyone has to learn to control the tongue. Staying mindful of the tremendous power of your words will help you think before you say something you might later regret.

Practice positive communication by speaking words of encouragement, kindness, and love to the people in your life. Make sure the tone of your voice and the expression on your face communicate the same message, for often they speak louder than words. You can find something positive to say about everyone—so make a point to do so.

Finally, the powers of darkness love to tangle up the lines of communication, so ask questions. This will eliminate a great deal of misunderstanding and help to head off strife before it begins.

In short, your words contain power. Purpose to speak ones that produce life, and you will have a positive impact everywhere you go.

Your loving Father

Compassion

Praise be to the . . . Father of compassion and the God of all
comfort, who comforts us in all our troubles, so that we can
comfort those in any trouble with the comfort we ourselves
have received from God.

2 CORINTHIANS 1:3-4

When Jesus went out He saw a great multitude; and He was
moved with compassion for them, and healed their sick.

MATTHEW 14:14 NKJV

Live in harmony with one another; be sympathetic, love as
brothers, be compassionate.

1 PETER 3:8

Jesus said, "You must be compassionate,
just as your Father is compassionate."

LUKE 6:36 NLT

God is fair; he will not forget the work you did and the love
you showed for him by helping his people. And he will
remember that you are still helping them.

HEBREWS 6:10 NCV

[Jehovah] is good to everyone, and his compassion is inter-
twined with everything he does.

PSALM 145:9 TLB

THE GREAT SHOE EXCHANGE

Pumps or platforms, moccasins or Manolos, ballet shoes or tattered tennies, work boots or orthopedic loafers—it's good to walk a mile in another's shoes now and then. But if all you do is momentarily empathize with someone's struggles and then walk away without doing anything, you have not allowed compassion to do its job.

Over and over again, compassion led Jesus to act. Seeing a widow mourning the death of her son moved Jesus to raise him from the dead (Luke 7:12-15). Feeling the tug at His robe of a woman who had suffered long and much, Jesus cured not only her body, but also her heart (Luke 8:43-48). Glimpsing the significance of a tiny child, Jesus took time out to hold her instead of treating her as a distraction (Matt. 19:13-15).

Jesus did more than put Himself in another's shoes. He donned human form. He experienced pain, sorrow, and rejection, so we can never accuse Him of not understanding how we feel. His compassion led Him to act on our behalf—to say yes to the cross so we could say yes to eternal life.

The next time you feel compassion tugging at your heart, answer with a resounding yes. Give generously of your time, your resources, and your energy. But most of all, give of your heart. Ask God what part you should play in aiding someone in need. Your part may be as simple as weeping with those who weep or offering a heartfelt prayer on another's behalf. When you allow God's compassion to flow through you into the lives of others, you'll not only help change their lives for the better, but your own as well.

Confidence

From one man he made every nation. . . . He determined the times set for them and the exact places where they should live.
ACTS 17:26

The Fear-of-God builds up confidence.
PROVERBS 14:26 MSG

O Lord GOD, You are my confidence.
PSALM 71:5 NASB

The LORD will be your confidence
and will keep your foot from being snared.
PROVERBS 3:26

The fruit of righteousness will be peace;
the effect of righteousness will be quietness and
confidence forever.
ISAIAH 32:17

It is better to trust the LORD
than to put confidence in people.
PSALM 118:8 NLT

ASSURED AND SECURE

You are entirely accepted and eternally loved by the same God who calls every star by name and who always has been and always will be. This Creator, Father, and Friend has crafted you with care and creativity—not only for His enjoyment but so you can make a positive impact on the world during this specific time in history. He has given you a unique place and purpose no one else can fill—along with a dynamic blend of talents, character traits, physical qualities, and personal experiences.

God promises not only never to leave you, but that His own Spirit will live inside you, guiding you and giving you strength, comfort, and wisdom as you go through each day. Anytime you call to Him, He is there—ready to listen and respond, ready to help you, heal you, and hold you close. No person, no circumstance, and no sin can ever separate you from His side.

Refuse to let the words of others shatter your confidence if their words contradict what God says is true. You are significant, beautiful, and deeply cherished. Place your confidence in this truth instead of the opinions of those around you.

At times, circumstances may shake your confidence in yourself and in the one in whom you have put your faith. When that happens, take your eyes off the externals for a moment and refocus on what's eternal: God and His promises. Recall the truth of who God is and who you are because of Him. This truth is strong enough to cut short any crisis in confidence you may face.

Contentment

He satisfies the longing soul,
And fills the hungry soul with goodness.

PSALM 107:9 NKJV

Be content with such things as ye have: for he hath said,
I will never leave thee, nor forsake thee.

HEBREWS 13:5 KJV

I have learned how to get along happily whether I have much or
little. I know how to live on almost nothing or with everything.
I have learned the secret of contentment in every situation.

PHILIPPIANS 4:11-12 TLB

Godliness with contentment is great gain. . . . If we have food and
clothing, we will be content with that.

1 TIMOTHY 6:6,8

The fear of the LORD leads to life:
Then one rests content, untouched by trouble.

PROVERBS 19:23

Prayer

Heavenly Father,

Contentment: What does that really feel like? I've experienced limited amounts of it, but I always have an underlying hunger for something more, something that truly satisfies.

I've noticed that when I become restless, I begin to yearn for things like a new outfit, a meaningful relationship, or—I hate to admit it— something as simple as a chocolate milkshake. Each of those things gives me a lift, but when the new wears off or my belly is empty again, that same restlessness returns. It seems as if I'm caught in an endless cycle, and I can see that it is futile.

Your Word says that the apostle Paul learned to be content. Do you think it is possible for me?

Amen.

HEART HUNGER

If you're the kind of woman who can shop 'til you drop, you know a lot about contentment. You know how good it feels to get something that looks great on you and is on sale to boot. But you also know that warm, fuzzy feeling of satisfaction doesn't last for long. You may enjoy your new purchase for a while, but pretty soon the call of the mall is going to lead you on a search for that next great buy.

Whether you like to shop or not, every woman knows what it feels like to long for something—to feel that ache in her soul that says, *Something's missing. My life's incomplete.* You may try to quench this empty feeling by filling your closet, your stomach, your ego, or your relational dance card. But contentment, the kind that lasts, can be sustained by only one thing—by the God who created the hole in your soul in the first place.

God created you with a longing for more than this life can offer. That longing is designed to lead you to Him. When you try to satisfy that longing with anything other than God, discontent is sure to follow. Treat discontent like a hunger pain. When you feel it, recognize you are craving more of God. Instead of running to the mall, spend time talking to Him. Thank Him for what He's provided for you today. Freely ask Him to meet your needs, but also ask Him to help you distinguish your needs from your wants. The more you fill your life with God and His love, the fewer "wants" you'll find yourself longing to fill.

Precious Child,

The longing of the human heart is something common to every person, for there is a God-shaped hole in every heart. You see, I created people in order to develop a relationship with them. The way that only a certain key will turn a lock, I am the only thing that will fit the opening and unlock the human heart to experience a life of love, joy, peace, and contentment.

People try all sorts of "keys" to satisfy their longings, but sooner or later they realize that, although they experience a limited amount of satisfaction, those keys don't really fit—and disappointment sets in.

I am happy for My people to have the desires of their hearts, but it is only as you seek Me first that these other things can fall into their proper places. Let Me satisfy your heart hunger; then you can truly enjoy these other things.

Your loving Father

Courage

Keep alert, stand firm in your faith,
be courageous, be strong.
1 CORINTHIANS 16:13 NRSV

Don't lose your courage or be afraid. Don't panic or be
frightened, because the LORD your God goes with you, to
fight for you against your enemies and to save you.
DEUTERONOMY 20:3-4 NCV

Be strong in the Lord and in the power of His might.
Put on the whole armor of God, that you may be able to
stand against the wiles of the devil.
EPHESIANS 6:10-11 NKJV

LORD, you are my shield,
my wonderful God who gives me courage.
PSALM 3:3 NCV

Do not lose the courage you had in the past, which has a great
reward. You must hold on, so you can do what God wants
and receive what he has promised.
HEBREWS 10:35-36 NCV

Be strong and courageous. Do not be afraid
or terrified . . . for the LORD your God goes with you;
he will never leave you nor forsake you.
DEUTERONOMY 31:6

RISKING IT ALL

A year of beauty treatments, a wardrobe filled with the finest gowns in the land, residence in the court of the king: to every onlooker under King Xerxes' reign, it looks as though Esther has won more than the king's beauty pageant to choose a new queen. It seems Esther is living a dream come true. But this isn't Esther's dream. It's God's. He is the One who has brought her to this place at this time. It isn't time for pageantry and pleasure. It's time for action—action that may end in her death.

Esther's heart races as her maids plait her rich russet hair. She has already risked death by entering the king's presence uninvited. Tonight, she will risk it again by revealing her heritage, hidden from the king until now. She will hold her head high and tell him she's a Jew. She will declare the same faith—and thereby the same fate—as all of the Jewish people the king has condemned to death. Esther prays, along with the rest of her people, that the king will be kind, that he will lift the edict, that tonight a dream will come true for every Jew in the land.

God's purpose prevailed that night through one woman who put everything in jeopardy for a godly cause. That doesn't mean Esther was unafraid. Without fear, courage is unnecessary. But when you are afraid, follow Esther's example. Place your trust in God's power and purpose for your life. Then, hold your head high and do what you know needs to be done.

Daily Walk

Your life is a journey you must travel with a deep
consciousness of God. It cost God plenty to get you out of
that dead-end, empty-headed life you grew up in.
He paid with Christ's sacred blood, you know.

1 PETER 1:17-19 MSG

God, who got you started in this spiritual adventure,
shares with us the life of his Son and our Master Jesus.
He will never give up on you. Never forget that.

1 CORINTHIANS 1:9 MSG

Your word is a lamp to my feet
And a light to my path.

PSALM 119:105 NASB

The path of the righteous is like the first gleam of dawn,
shining ever brighter till the full light of day.

PROVERBS 4:18

Lead me in the right path, O LORD, . . .
Tell me clearly what to do,
and show me which way to turn.

PSALM 5:8 NLT

THE JOURNEY OF A LIFETIME

Today you will take part in a journey, even if you never venture outside the front door of your home. It's a journey that won't be measured in miles or sunsets or photo album pages. It can't be charted on a map or booked on the Internet. Nonetheless, this journey will lead you where your heart longs to go. It will lead you closer to God.

Your path may feel uncertain at times—the road, rough or uneven. Some days, it may appear you've reached a dead end. On others, you'll happen upon a landscape so breathtaking that tears of wonder will stream down your cheeks. If you keep your eyes open, you'll find that every day, no matter what your path looks like, will offer you the opportunity to move forward, to find new adventures on both familiar and distant shores.

As with any journey you take, it's vitally important to first make sure you're headed in the right direction. So each morning, check out your landmarks. Look for direction and insight by reading God's words in the Bible. Take a few moments to talk to God in prayer. Look back over where you traveled the day before and talk with God about anything you wish you'd done differently. Ask Him to help lead you today to make decisions that will draw you closer to Him. Then, venture out into the world with confidence.

God has the itinerary for your life held firmly in His hand. Today is yet one more step on the journey He has planned for you to take together—an adventure that will last throughout eternity.

Doubt

Lord, when doubts fill my mind, when my heart is in turmoil,
quiet me and give me renewed hope and cheer.

PSALM 94:19 TLB

Jesus said, "Anything is possible if a person believes." The father
instantly replied, "I do believe, but help me not to doubt!"

MARK 9:23-24 NLT

Faith comes from hearing the message,
and the message is heard through the word of Christ.

ROMANS 10:17

He has given us both his promise and his oath,
two things we can completely count on, for it is impossible
for God to tell a lie. Now all those who flee to him to save them can
take new courage when they hear such assurances from God;
now they can know without doubt that he will give them
the salvation he has promised them.

HEBREWS 6:18 TLB

Be merciful to those who doubt.

JUDE 1:22 TLB

Heavenly Father,

I hate to admit it, but sometimes the Bible character I most identify with is doubting Thomas. I want to believe, Father, but the thoughts in my head and the circumstances that surround me drown out the voice of faith that is struggling to gain ascendancy in my heart.

I'm amazed when I see how effortlessly faith comes to some people. They just take Your Word at face value and that settles the issue for them. It is enough to banish their fears and overcome their doubts, but I'm just not there yet.

Your Word tells me that faith is what pleases You, Father, and I desire to change from doubting to believing. Is there any hope for me? Will You help me grow in this area?

Amen.

UNFOCUSED VIEW

God knows your doubts. He knows what you struggle to believe in and what you can't quite comprehend, but He doesn't hold any of that against you. He is fully aware of your humanity and your frailty, your finite brain and your distracted heart. Yet, He still wants you to know Him and believe Him—even if you can't fully grasp the whole picture of who He is.

God is so big that He doesn't fully fit within the frame of the human mind. His infinite presence, perfect plans, divine purposes, and eternal perspective are more than your brain can hold. While you're here on earth, you can see only one small part of God's portrait. You may have a fairly clear view of His power or His creativity, but perhaps His righteousness or His grace seem a bit fuzzy from where you're standing. The view others have may differ a bit from your own. What they claim to see clearly may be blocked from your view. They may feel certain about things you may doubt, or they may question areas that you feel are settled and secure in your own mind.

Sharing your doubts and your beliefs with others can help you both grow—as long as you don't end up debating the details of what cannot yet be fully understood. Instead of focusing on your doubts, focus on what you do know about God. The wisdom of God's Spirit, the Bible, your personal experience, and the insights of others can all help broaden your view of your heavenly Father. They can bring the parts of the picture you can see into a finer, richer, more beautiful focus.

My Precious Child,

Of course I will help you! What you are experiencing is a common human frailty, and that is why I've included the stories of ordinary people in My Word to encourage you and help you grow.

When Thomas doubted, Jesus encouraged him to touch His side to see that He was alive and well. When Peter walked on the water and then began to doubt and sink, Jesus reached out, took Peter by the hand, and lifted him up. Peter's doubt overtook his faith, but over time he became a mighty man of faith.

I will do the same for you. Meditate on scriptures that pertain to the situations you are facing and see yourself with the desired result. Then when doubts come knocking, let My Word answer the door and silence them.

Your loving Father

Emotions

A sound mind makes for a robust body,
but runaway emotions corrode the bones.
PROVERBS 14:30 MSG

Churned milk turns into butter;
riled emotions turn into fist fights.
PROVERBS 30:33 MSG

We use our powerful God-tools for . . . tearing down
barriers erected against the truth of God, fitting every loose
thought and emotion and impulse into the structure of life
shaped by Christ.
2 CORINTHIANS 10:5 MSG

Do you see a man who is hasty in his words?
There is more hope for a fool than for him.
PROVERBS 29:20 NASB

It is not good to have zeal without knowledge,
nor to be hasty and miss the way.
PROVERBS 19:2

EMOTIONAL BALANCE

Rhoda jumps to her feet, startled by the knock on the door. As a servant, it's her job to welcome those who arrive at the outer gate—yet she hesitates. Afraid of who's concealed behind the door, she pictures King Herod's soldiers. An involuntary shudder shakes her small frame.

Fear sends her thoughts racing. Perhaps the soldiers are here to drag away everyone inside who's gathered to pray for Peter's release from prison. Her heart pounds as she gathers the courage to call out timidly, "Who's there?"

The voice that answers shakes Rhoda more deeply than the answer of a soldier's command. It's Peter! Alive and free! Our prayers have been answered! In her excitement, Rhoda runs to tell the others the miraculous news—forgetting to open the door and invite Peter inside!

Just like Rhoda, you may let emotions push you to act before you think. They can incite your thoughts to run ahead and write scenarios inspired more by fear or fantasy than fact. However, God designed your emotions to be a gift, not a shortcoming. They can warn you of danger, energize you with joy, and inspire you to serve others. Just remember to balance your emotions by lining them up with God's truth. Keep facts ahead of your feelings. Pray for the discernment to know when your emotions are coming on too strong. Then use both your heart and your mind to act wisely in whatever situation you face today.

Encouragement

Anxious hearts are very heavy but
a word of encouragement does wonders!
PROVERBS 12:25 TLB

Encourage one another daily, as long as it is called Today,
so that none of you may be hardened by sin's deceitfulness.
HEBREWS 3:13

Encourage each other.
Live in harmony and peace.
2 CORINTHIANS 13:11 NLT

Why are you downcast, O my soul?
Why so disturbed within me?
Put your hope in God,
for I will yet praise him,
my Savior and my God.
PSALM 43:5

David was greatly distressed; for the people spake of stoning
him, because the soul of all the people was grieved, every man
for his sons and for his daughters: but David
encouraged himself in the LORD his God.
1 SAMUEL 30:6 KJV

ON THE ROAD AGAIN

Everyone can use a little roadside assistance along the highway of life. At times, the journey can feel long. Certain stretches may seem lonely, monotonous, or dangerous. Some days may be uncomfortably bumpy, while others hold terrain that looks so unfamiliar you may fear you've lost your way. At times such as these, a little encouragement can go a long way: a note from a friend, a message on your voice mail that simply says, "I love you," a hug when words aren't enough, a pat on the back from someone you look up to, an unexpected gift, a heartfelt smile, a timely word.

When you receive a gift of encouragement such as this, cherish it. Let the warmth of it surround your soul like an embrace. Thank God for the generosity of the one who has extended it to you. Learn from his or her example so you can grow more skillful in encouraging others when they need a little roadside assistance.

But know there will be times when you find yourself in need of an uplifting, encouraging word—and no one will be there to extend it to you. At least that's how it will look at first glance. However, God has given you enough encouragement to take you through this lifetime and into the next. When your heart needs a lift, lift up God's Word. Read, reread, meditate on, and memorize your favorite verses. You'll find these words of hope and healing have the power to lift your heart and your spirits, no matter how heavy they may be.

Eternal Life

Jesus said . . . , "I am the resurrection and the life;
he who believes in Me will live even if he dies, and everyone who
lives and believes in Me will never die."

JOHN 11:25-26 NASB

Jesus said, "I came so they can have real and eternal life,
more and better life than they ever dreamed of."

JOHN 10:10 MSG

Jesus said, "This is eternal life: that they may know you,
the only true God, and Jesus Christ, whom you have sent."

JOHN 17:3

Jesus said, "Very truly, I tell you, anyone who hears my word and
believes him who sent me has eternal life, and does not come under
judgment, but has passed from death to life."

JOHN 5:24 NRSV

This is the testimony: God gave us eternal life, and this life is in
his Son. Whoever has the Son has life; whoever does not have the
Son of God does not have life.

1 JOHN 5:11-12 NRSV

Heavenly Father,

Oh, how I wish there were a fountain of youth. Some days I look in the mirror and it's as though I've aged overnight. They call them "laugh lines," but to me they are anything but funny. Also as I've gotten older, I'm finding it harder and harder to keep my body looking young and fit. I don't have to look far to see perfect faces and perfect bodies; the media has seen to that. Whatever happened to growing old gracefully? It's an uphill battle and sometimes it's just overwhelming.

Lord, I don't want to be vain, and I ask You to forgive me for falling into that trap. It's just that life is flying by so rapidly that I hardly know where the years are going. Help me keep my focus on You and on the things that really matter—life spent with You throughout eternity.

Amen.

LIFE QUEST

In the third century AD, alchemists in China searched diligently for an elixir that would prolong life, perhaps indefinitely. Ironically, what they wound up creating was gunpowder—more of an elixir for a quick death than a long life.[4] But their search was not an isolated case. From the elaborate burial and mummification process of the ancient Egyptians to Ponce de León's exploration for the fountain of youth to the modern-day option of preserving your body through cryogenics—the quest for a life-giving elixir has continued throughout history right up to present day. Yet all of these quests have ended up the same way the alchemists' experiments ended—in death, not life.

There is only one genuine elixir for lasting life. It's found in the divine and historical person of Jesus Christ. He is the only One throughout history who promised to hold the key to eternal life and then rose from the dead to provide living proof that everything He said was true. Jesus holds out this same life-giving key as a free gift to every person who believes that He is who He says He is. The much-sought-after elixir of life is within your reach.

As with every person, your time here on earth can be measured. It has a beginning, and one day it will come to an end. But thanks to Jesus, your lifeline doesn't end there. Death is just a brief intermission. The main feature is yet to come: a life, the length of which cannot be measured, spent in the company of One whose love for you will never fade.

Dear, Dear Daughter,

The reason that everyone clamors for a youthful appearance and long life is that I created the human spirit to live forever. I never intended for people to grow old and die. That phenomenon took hold when Adam sinned, and the earth became corrupted as a result. But even with Adam's fatal mistake, I have made a way by which all can experience everlasting life. It is through the death, burial, and resurrection of My Son. Whoever receives Him receives His life and will never die spiritually.

Unfortunately, the human body continues to grow older by the day—but the human spirit, when born again and filled with My life, is renewed day by day. That is what salvation is all about. Someday in heaven, all of My children will receive a glorified body, but until then, eternal life is yours for the taking.

Your loving Father

Expectations

The Lord God says:
". . . Anyone who trusts in me will not be disappointed."
ISAIAH 49:22-23 NCV

The Lord God says:
"I will put a stone in the ground in Jerusalem,
a tested stone. Everything will be built on this important
and precious rock. Anyone who trusts in it
will never be disappointed."
ISAIAH 28:16 NCV

My soul, wait thou only upon God;
for my expectation is from him.
PSALM 62:5 KJV

To Him who is able to do exceedingly abundantly above all
that we ask or think, according to the power that works in us,
to Him be glory in the church by Christ Jesus.
EPHESIANS 3:20-21 NKJV

As for me, I will watch expectantly for the LORD;
I will wait for the God of my salvation.
MICAH 7:7 NASB

GREAT EXPECTATIONS

What expectations do you have for your life? A fulfilling career? Marriage? Motherhood? Home ownership? Popularity? The body of a supermodel? Taking a frank look at the differences between what you hope to experience in life and what you whole-heartedly expect God will bring your way can mean the difference between contentment and resentment.

God promises you many things. One of them is that He will meet your needs—but those needs are determined by an all-wise God who knows you and loves you better than you do yourself, not by your own fickle dreams of what you think is a perfect life. God will fulfill many of your deepest desires along the way—and even bring to life some dreams you didn't dare to dream—but the story He has planned for you may look different from the one you have been writing in your head since childhood.

Go ahead and expect good things from God. Expect that He will bring good out of every circumstance. Expect that He will work in your life to make your character more like His. Expect that His love for you will never fail or change. Expect Him to keep His Word. Expect to spend eternity in His presence. But as for the details of life, share your longings and desires openly with Him. Then, allow Him to sort and sift them, bringing His very best to you in the way that He sees fit. In the end, you'll discover joy and contentment that will exceed your greatest expectations.

Faith

What is faith? It is the confident assurance that what we hope for is going to happen. It is the evidence of things we cannot yet see.

HEBREWS 11:1 NLT

[Abraham] did not waver at the promise of God through unbelief, but was strengthened in faith, giving glory to God, and being fully convinced that what He had promised He was also able to perform.

ROMANS 4:20-21 NKJV

We walk by faith, not by sight.

2 CORINTHIANS 5:7 KJV

What good is it, my brothers, if a man claims to have faith but has no deeds? Can such faith save him? Suppose a brother or sister is without clothes and daily food. If one of you says to him, "Go, I wish you well; keep warm and well fed," but does nothing about his physical needs, what good is it? In the same way, faith by itself, if it is not accompanied by action, is dead. But someone will say, "You have faith; I have deeds." Show me your faith without deeds, and I will show you my faith by what I do.

JAMES 2:14-18

ONE ACT OF FAITH

The coarsely woven red curtain that separates Rahab's room from the rest of the house is held to one side by a frayed scarlet cord. She pulls the simple adornment free with a gentle tug of her hand. Usually the unfurled curtain means she doesn't want to be disturbed, that a client is sharing her bed. But today, this cord holds Rahab's future. It holds life for her, her family, and future generations. She ties the cord so it hangs out her window, dangling down Jericho's massive city wall. From outside the city, the cord looks like a thin, red scar on a cold, stone face.

Rahab's lie to the king's messengers has ensured the safe passage of the Israelite spies back to their army. Lying isn't anything new for Rahab, considering her profession. But what is new is her faith in this foreign God. She's heard the stories—stories of a God so powerful that He held back the Red Sea so His people could escape from the slavery of Pharaoh's iron grip. And now God's army is headed for Jericho (Josh. 2:1-21). Her only hope is to call on this God of Moses and Joshua—to call on Him to also become the God of Rahab.

Faith begins with one act of trust. Rahab put her trust in an unknown God because she believed His power could save her. The cord was her covenant with the spies, assuring herself and her family safe passage. But it was also a covenant with God—a visible sign that declared, "I believe."

True faith always leads to action. Where will your faith lead you today?

Faithfulness

Women . . . must be serious, not slanderers,
but temperate, faithful in all things.
1 TIMOTHY 3:11 NRSV

A talebearer revealeth secrets: but he that is of a faithful spirit
concealeth the matter.
PROVERBS 11:13 KJV

How thankful I am to Christ Jesus our Lord for
. . . giving me the strength to be faithful to him.
1 TIMOTHY 1:12 TLB

If we are faithful to the end,
trusting God just as we did when we first became Christians,
we will share in all that belongs to Christ.
HEBREWS 3:14 TLB

Oh, love the LORD, all you His saints!
For the LORD preserves the faithful.
PSALM 31:23 NKJV

O Jehovah, Commander of the heavenly armies,
where is there any other Mighty One like you?
Faithfulness is your very character.
PSALM 89:8 TLB

Heavenly Father,

I think I understand what Jesus meant when He said that the spirit is willing but the flesh is weak. That accurately describes me in many ways. I truly mean to be faithful to my promises, to be someone others can count on, to be someone You can count on—but the reality is that I sometimes fall short. I intend to spend time with You every morning, but when my eyelids get heavy, I often hit the snooze button and fall back to sleep. I mean well when I volunteer to help out at church, but I sometimes let other things get in the way and I let people down. I want to be a faithful friend, but I've sometimes missed it there as well.

Help me to be more like You, Father. You are faithful no matter what, and I want that to be said of me too.

Amen.

A RELATIONALLY HEALTHY HABIT

When you're scheduled for your regular cleaning and checkup at the dentist, chances are you scrub your teeth right before you head out the door. You may even get out the floss and swish around a little mouthwash. But once you arrive at the dentist's office, the truth becomes clear. Your teeth and gums tell the real story as to whether you've been faithful with your oral hygiene or not.

Faithfully brushing, flossing, and cleaning your teeth helps maintain your oral health. Faithfully telling the truth, keeping your promises, and maintaining your integrity will help maintain your relational health. Only coming through half the time on actually doing what you say you'll do is like brushing your teeth only a couple of days a week. You'll wind up with holes in your relationships as surely as you will cavities in your teeth.

God is the ultimate example of what it means to be faithful. He never reneges on His promises. He doesn't need excuses. His character remains steadfast and dependable, regardless of circumstances. Since you are created in God's image, faithfulness is something that should be readily evident in your character as well. If you asked your friends, your family, your coworkers, your boss, your neighbors, and God himself about how reliable and faithful they think you are, how do you think they'd respond?

If there are some areas in your life that are developing plaque from inattention, ask God to help you cultivate a healthy habit of faithfulness, beginning today. Don't settle for having the best of intentions. Be a woman who is true to her word and her true character.

Precious Child,

Yes, faithfulness is part of My character, and because I live in you, you, too, can be faithful. One way to safeguard yourself is not to commit to things without first thinking through all of the ramifications. It's tempting to say yes when requests are made of you, but it is far better not to commit than to commit and let others down.

I know you strive to be faithful, and it blesses My heart. Realize that all people fall short on occasion, but I offer you forgiveness and the chance to try again. Don't hesitate to come to Me when you blow it, and be quick to make things right with others when you fail to follow through.

Faithfulness is a fruit of the Spirit, and when you allow that fruit to mature in you, you honor Me and reveal My character to those around you.

Your loving Father

Fear

Don't be afraid, for I am with you. Do not be dismayed,
for I am your God. I will strengthen you. I will help you.
I will uphold you with my victorious right hand.

ISAIAH 41:10 NLT

When I am afraid, I will put my confidence in you.
Yes, I will trust the promises of God.

PSALM 56:3-4 TLB

God has not given us a spirit of fear,
but of power and of love and of a sound mind.

2 TIMOTHY 1:7 NKJV

The LORD is for me; I will not fear;
What can man do to me?

PSALM 118:6 NASB

I am the LORD, your God,
who takes hold of your right hand
and says to you, Do not fear;
I will help you.

ISAIAH 41:13

FEAR FACTORS

What are you afraid of? Research shows that the majority of the population suffers from glossophobia, the fear of public speaking. Other common phobias are the fear of flying (aviophobia), falling (acrophobia), or being trapped in a small space (claustrophobia). On the more obscure side, there are people who actually suffer from arachibutyrophobia, which is the fear of having peanut butter stuck to the roof of their mouths or even hippopotomonstros-esquippedaliophobia, which is, understandably, the fear of long words.

But when you are really afraid, regardless of whether others think your fear is valid or not, the situation is anything but humorous. Fear can make your heart pound and your palms sweat. It can make you turn and run the other way. Or, if you are concerned about keeping your cool in public, fear can simply make you avoid situations where you might happen to meet your fears face-to-face. That means that on the road map of life, fear can force you to take a detour. It can keep you from going the direction God wants you to go.

Throughout the Bible, people are reminded to "fear not" because God is with them. That message is just as true for you today. God is near. Call on Him when you're afraid, instead of hightailing it the other direction. Ask God to help you sort out what is rational and what is not. Instead of letting your thoughts tie your emotions in knots, concentrate on how big and powerful God is in light of what you fear. Then, keep moving forward with your head held high. You're not alone.

Forgiveness

Bear with each other and forgive
whatever grievances you may have against one another.
Forgive as the LORD forgave you.
COLOSSIANS 3:13

Forgive one another as quickly and thoroughly as
God in Christ forgave you.
EPHESIANS 4:32 MSG

Jesus said, "When you stand praying, if you hold anything
against anyone, forgive him, so that your Father in heaven
may forgive you your sins."
MARK 11:25

Peter came to Jesus and asked, "Lord, when my fellow believer
sins against me, how many times must I forgive him? Should
I forgive him as many as seven times?" Jesus answered, "I tell
you, you must forgive him more than seven times. You must
forgive him even if he does wrong to you seventy times seven."
MATTHEW 18:21-22 NCV

A further reason for forgiveness is to keep from being
outsmarted by Satan; for we know what he is trying to do.
2 CORINTHIANS 2:11 TLB

THE FIRST STONE

The door bursts open, inviting a sharp sword of daylight to slice through the darkness. Shouts and accusations fill the once-quiet room as rough hands pull the woman out of bed. She looks up to see her lover fleeing into another room. She hastily grabs the bedsheet as she's dragged through the open door. She has to have something to cover herself, something besides her own fear and shame.

"Stone her!" a religious leader cries out from the crowd at the temple nearby. It seems a just punishment, one condoned by the Law of Moses. After all, everyone knows what kind of woman she is. She was caught in bed with her lover, a man who was not her husband. Angry words echo off the walls of the temple courtyard, falling on the woman like physical blows.

Amid the chaos, one Man remains quiet. Despite the fact that the Pharisees are pushing Him for an answer as to what should be done, He bends down to the ground. Like a distracted child, He writes with His finger in the sand. As the leaders begin to lose patience, the Man says simply, "Let the person who has never done anything wrong throw the first stone" (John 8:7).

One by one, from the oldest to the youngest, the men disappear into the shadows, until only the Teacher and the woman are left. Jesus says to her gently, "If they don't condemn you, neither do I."

Every person on earth lives an imperfect life—one in need of forgiveness. When you're faced with someone who's hurt you, choose to extend the same gift of forgiveness that Jesus has so freely extended to you.

Freedom

Jesus said, "If the Son makes you free,
you will be free indeed."

JOHN 8:36 RSV

It was for freedom that Christ set us free;
therefore keep standing firm and
do not be subject again to a yoke of slavery.

GALATIANS 5:1 NASB

We know that our old life died with Christ on the cross
so that our sinful selves would have no power over us
and we would not be slaves to sin.

ROMANS 6:6 NCV

Jesus said, "If you continue in my word, you are truly my disciples,
and you will know the truth, and the truth will make you free."

JOHN 8:31-32 RSV

It is absolutely clear that God has called you to a free life.
Just make sure that you don't use this freedom as an excuse
to do whatever you want to do and destroy your freedom.
Rather, use your freedom to serve one another in love;
that's how freedom grows.

GALATIANS 5:13 MSG

Heavenly Father,

I long to experience the freedom You talk about in Your Word. I believe it when Jesus said that I would know the truth and that it would set me free, but so far that has not been my experience. Whom the Son sets free is free indeed. How do I get there from here?

Some of the things that hold me back—guilt, fear of failure, fear of what others think, shame—do I need to go on? My heart's desire is to break free from these chains that bind me. It's the only way I will ever reach my full potential and fulfill Your plan for my life. I need Your help, Father.

Amen.

✦

BORN TO BE WILD

You may not be aware of it, but you could be a woman held captive—a slave to something you can't even see. Not all chains are visible. There may be restraints digging into your heart, instead of your wrists—shackles holding you back from venturing farther down the road God has set before you. You may strain against them, but the invisible links that inhibit your freedom are forged from sturdy stuff, such as habits, heartbreak, bitterness, and pride. Self-effort cannot break them. Time cannot weaken them. Only God can release you from them—yet you hold the key.

Do you want to be free? You may be thinking, *What a crazy question! Who wouldn't want to be free?* But freedom can be heady stuff. Like a zoo animal which is offered freedom yet chooses to return to the comfort of his cage, you may find it easy to venture out to follow God yet return to old habits because they feel safe and familiar. The freedom God offers is vast and wild. It will take you places you've never dreamed you'd go. It will stir your passions and make you face your fears. It will challenge you to become the woman God had in mind when He knit you together in your mother's womb (Ps. 139:13).

If you're ready for that kind of freedom—for that level of adventure—allow God to turn the key you hold in your hand. Choose to drop the chains that are holding you back, to walk away from them once and for all. Choose to walk with God, following His road map for life every day.

Precious Child,

The first thing you need to realize is that you have an enemy who is bent on holding you captive. He constantly whispers in your ear those things that dampen your spirit, prevent you from trying new things, keep you from obeying Me, and hinder you from doing many of the things your heart longs for.

Realize that he is a liar and the father of lies so nothing that he says to you is true. As you submit yourself to Me by feeding on My Word and building up your spirit, you will find you have the power to resist him and to overcome every obstacle he throws your way. I have a tremendous plan for your life, and through Christ, you can realize your full potential, leaving the chains of bondage behind.

Your loving Father

Friendship

A friend loveth at all times.
PROVERBS 17:17 KJV

As iron sharpens iron, a friend sharpens a friend.
PROVERBS 27:17 NLT

The eye cannot say to the hand, "I have no need of you,"
nor again the head to the feet, "I have no need of you."
On the contrary, the parts of the body which
seem to be weaker are indispensable.
1 CORINTHIANS 12:21-22 RSV

Jesus said, "This is my commandment,
that you love one another as I have loved you.
No one has greater love than this, to lay down one's life
for one's friends."
JOHN 15:12-13 NRSV

Accept one another, then, just as Christ accepted you.
ROMANS 15:7

Confess your sins to each other and pray for each other
so that you may be healed.
JAMES 5:16 NLT

HAND IN HAND, HEART-TO-HEART

God is good. He is always near. He loves you beyond anything you can imagine. But sometimes you need a companion with skin on—someone whose smile you can see, laugh you can hear, and hug you can feel. When God first created the world, He acknowledged that it wasn't good for people to be alone (Gen. 2:18). That truth still holds true today.

It isn't good for you to live life on your own. You need a circle of friends who will accept you for who you are today, yet encourage you toward becoming the woman you will mature into tomorrow. The size of your circle doesn't matter. What matters is the love and authenticity that hold it together.

Nurture the friends you already have in your life. Show your love for them in ways that feed their soul. Lean on them when you need it, and allow them to do the same with you. Take time to celebrate milestones and accomplishments in each other's lives. Be honest but kind at the same time, speaking words that help and heal. Allow each other room to breathe, yet stay close enough to know when a friend could use your help—before she even has to ask.

At the same time, always be on the lookout for future friends waiting in the wings. A new coworker, the neighbor down the street, or the stranger sitting next to you in church could turn out to be someone who will help you discover just how beautiful the word *friend* can be.

Generosity

Let each one [give] as he has made up his own mind and purposed in his heart, not reluctantly or sorrowfully or under compulsion, for God loves (He takes pleasure in, prizes above other things, and is unwilling to abandon or to do without) a cheerful (joyous, "prompt to do it") giver [whose heart is in his giving].

2 CORINTHIANS 9:7 AMP

It is good to be merciful and generous.
Those who are fair in their business
will never be defeated.
Good people will always be remembered.

PSALM 112:5-6 NCV

A generous person will be enriched,
and one who gives water will get water.

PROVERBS 11:25 NRSV

You will be enriched in every way for great generosity.

2 CORINTHIANS 9:11 RSV

Good people will be generous to others and
will be blessed for all they do.

ISAIAH 32:8 NLT

TWO·COIN TREASURE

The widow's threadbare robe stands out like a blemish among the finery of the others in line. So do the lines on the old woman's face, deeply carved into her cheeks and forehead by years of heavy toil under the hot Middle Eastern sun. Yet her olive-colored eyes are still clear, vibrantly alive, making her seem like a young girl who has simply donned the disguise of an impoverished old woman. Her half-crooked smile seems to confirm the charade, giving the impression that at any time it could break into laughter or song.

Instead, the woman empties the contents of her worn leather pouch into her gnarled fingers—two small copper coins (Mark 12:41-44). They are all she has to live on. But the woman has seen God care for her in amazing ways in the past. Knowing how generous He's been to her, the widow feels she can be nothing less than joyfully generous in return.

Generosity is not determined by the size of a gift but by the size of the heart that extends it. Jesus commended the widow's donation of a couple of cents to aid the temple as worth more than the larger amounts of money that were given out of the excess wealth of the rich.

God can transform any gift you give into a bountiful blessing. Give generously of your money, your time, and your resources—whether you have much or little. When you freely open your heart and your hands in gratitude to God, you'll discover a fresh wealth of joy is suddenly yours.

Gentleness

My friends, if anyone is detected in a transgression,
you who have received the Spirit should restore such a one in a
spirit of gentleness. Take care that you yourselves are not tempted.

GALATIANS 6:1 NRSV

Are there those among you who are truly wise and understanding?
Then they should show it by living right and doing good things with
a gentleness that comes from wisdom.

JAMES 3:13 NCV

A soft answer turns away wrath, but harsh words cause quarrels.

PROVERBS 15:1 TLB

The Lord's servants must not quarrel but must be kind to everyone.
They must be . . . patient with difficult people. They should gently
teach those who oppose the truth. Perhaps God will change those
people's hearts, and they will believe the truth. Then they will come
to their senses and escape from the Devil's trap.

2 TIMOTHY 2:24-26 NLT

The wisdom that comes from heaven is first of all pure
and full of quiet gentleness.

JAMES 3:17 TLB

Heavenly Father,

One of the attributes I most appreciate about You is that You are gentle. The picture of Jesus being my gentle Shepherd never ceases to comfort me and make me feel safe in Your presence. I never have to fear that You will use sharp tones with me or abuse me in any way. How different that is from many earthly authority figures.

Whether I am in my role as a daughter, a mother, a boss, sister, or friend, I want the fruit of gentleness to be evident in my every word and action. Forgive me for those times that I grow impatient and demanding—harsh and insensitive —for it is at those times that I least reflect Your nature. Your gentleness makes all the difference in the world.

Amen.

GENTLE STRENGTH

God is well aware of His own strength and carefully chooses how to use it. He is immeasurably powerful, yet He is gentle enough to fashion a delicate butterfly or dry the invisible tears hidden inside a broken heart. God's gentleness doesn't make Him weak. Gentleness is strength under control—tempered by compassion, sensitivity, and wisdom. A burly football player tenderly cradling a newborn infant is a perfect picture of gentleness in action. However, a shy young woman tentatively tapping a gentleman on the shoulder to get his attention because she is too afraid to make her request aloud is not demonstrating gentleness—just timidity.

You can be gentle and still boldly share what you believe. You can be gentle and still stand your ground on important issues. You can be gentle and still refuse to be taken advantage of. All it takes on your part is a humble heart that is ready to listen and respond to others in a way that reflects God's own love.

Reach out in gentleness today. Listen well before you speak. Choose your words wisely, securing each with a ribbon of unconditional love. Think carefully before you act. Treat people the way you would your most precious, breakable treasures. Hold them securely yet gently with your attention, your words, your touch, and your prayers. Those around you, even those who put on a rough-and-tumble exterior, are still fragile. All humans are. They need to be handled with care—with the same gentleness God has shown you.

Precious Child,

Not only did I communicate that Jesus is the Good Shepherd, I also likened My children to sheep. It doesn't take a harsh individual to keep sheep in line—just gentle prodding and an occasional excursion to bring a wayward sheep home. This is the way I deal with you.

Just as I am gentle with you, you are to be gentle with others. When restoring a wayward believer, do it kindly. When you need help resolving a conflict, let peace prevail. When mistreated by others, draw on My gentle strength to see you through.

Doing things in your own power will usually result in stress, pressure, impatience, and harshness. Doing things in My strength will enable you to respond as Jesus did—gently.

Your loving Father

God's Faithfulness

I face your Temple as I worship, giving thanks to you for all
your lovingkindness and your faithfulness, for your promises
are backed by all the honor of your name.

PSALM 138:2 TLB

Lord, you are a God who shows mercy and is kind.
You don't become angry quickly.
You have great love and faithfulness.

PSALM 86:15 NCV

All the paths of the LORD are steadfast love and faithfulness,
for those who keep his covenant and his testimonies.

PSALM 25:10 RSV

Your love, O LORD, reaches to the heavens,
your faithfulness to the skies.

PSALM 36:5

Great is his steadfast love toward us;
and the faithfulness of the LORD endures for ever.

PSALM 117:2 RSV

TRUSTWORTHY AND TRUE

Old Faithful doesn't really live up to its name. There is a legend that started in the early days of Yellowstone Park that the geyser erupted every hour on the hour. However, the intervals between each eruption actually range from somewhere between 30 to 120 minutes, with eruptions lasting from ninety seconds to five minutes and the height of the water rising from 90 to 184 feet. The longer the eruption, the longer the interval until the next time she blows.[5]

One reason Old Faithful is considered so faithful is that so many people, both park rangers and visitors, pay attention to it. After years of watching it erupt, the pattern of its irregular regularity has become more predictable.

When you pay attention to God's faithfulness, you begin to appreciate just how reliable He really is. As with Old Faithful, God's timing will not always be in sync with your own. But as you wait for Him to act, you can rest in the fact that there's a lot going on beneath the surface that you cannot see. God, like Old Faithful, erupts into action only when conditions are just right.

As you actively watch for God's answers to prayer, take note of how He fulfills His promises, and read in the Bible about how God has come through for others in the past, your trust in Him will naturally grow, far beyond geyser tall.

God's Love

God is love. This is how God showed his love to us:
He sent his one and only Son into the world so that
we could have life through him.
1 JOHN 4:8-9 NCV

God shows his great love for us in this way:
Christ died for us while we were still sinners.
ROMANS 5:8 NCV

The LORD shows mercy and is kind.
He does not become angry quickly,
and he has great love.
PSALM 103:8 NCV

The Lord said,
"I have loved you with an everlasting love;
Therefore I have drawn you with lovingkindness."
JEREMIAH 31:3 NASB

Blessed be the LORD,
for he has wondrously shown his steadfast love to me.
PSLAAM 31:21 NRSV

How precious is your steadfast love, O God!
PSALM 36:7 NRSV

ONCE UPON ETERNITY

God's love transcends that of fairy tales. God is the faithful Suitor who follows you to the ends of the earth, waiting patiently for the day you'll return His affection; the courageous Warrior who fights to protect you from dangers you can't even see; the benevolent King who showers His beautiful bride with gifts that dazzle your imagination; the Knight in shining armor whose heart toward you is always pure and good; the handsome Prince who gives His life in exchange for yours.

God's love for you is not a romantic fantasy. It's as real as your next breath. The Scriptures say that God not only loves but that He is love itself. His essence, His very being, is a picture of what real love is like. He is a love that will never falter or fail, never hold grudges or point fingers, never grow old or out of touch, never take you for granted or use you for selfish gain. God is a love you can count on, forever and always.

Since God is love, He can love others besides you without diminishing the unique love story He is writing hand in hand with you. Together, you hold the pen. Your eternal biography is a collaboration between yourself and your true Soul Mate. Write your part with strokes of wonder, worship, and joy. Pen your questions, doubts, and fears. God's all-encompassing love can weave every word into a story worth living where your "happily ever after" is never in doubt.

God's Presence

The eternal God is a dwelling place,
And underneath are the everlasting arms.
DEUTERONOMY 33:27 NASB

Where can I flee from your presence?
. . . If I rise on the wings of the dawn,
if I settle on the far side of the sea,
even there your hand will guide me,
your right hand will hold me fast.
PSALM 139:7,9-10

Blessed are those who have learned to acclaim you,
who walk in the light of your presence, O LORD.
PSALM 89:15

You will show me the path of life;
In Your presence is fullness of joy;
At Your right hand are pleasures forevermore.
PSALM 16:11 NKJV

The LORD replied, "My Presence will go with you,
and I will give you rest."
EXODUS 33:14

Heavenly Father,

Sometimes I wish I could have lived when Jesus walked the earth. It seems as though believing would have been so much easier. I would have seen with my own eyes the miracles He performed. I would have heard with my own ears the powerful words He spoke.

I especially wish I could have lived during that time so that I could have experienced the warmth of His embrace, His very presence firsthand.

There are times when I have sensed Your presence, and when I have, everything earthly paled in comparison. I was more aware of You than any of the circumstances surrounding my life. I've tasted of Your goodness, Father, and I hunger for more of You and Your glorious presence.

Amen.

FOREVER BY YOUR SIDE

You're never alone. Someone who loves you is always near—in joy and in sorrow, in pleasure and in pain, in victory and in difficulty, in sickness and in health. Not even death can keep you two apart. No one but God can make that promise to you.

Your loving Father has His eyes on you and His arms around you day and night, year after year, from before you were born throughout the unfathomable reaches of eternity. You may not always feel His presence in the way you wish you could. At times you may be able to know He is near only because His steadfast promise tells you so. But as you get to know Him better, you'll be able to discern His presence in other, subtle ways: in the comforting embrace of an understanding friend, in His words of hope and healing found in Scripture, in the beauty of wildflowers glistening with morning dew, in the nudge in your heart to call someone in need only to discover she'd just finished asking God to send her someone such as you.

God is present and active and involved in every detail of your life. Picture Him with you right now. Climb into His lap. Put your tiny hands in the palms of the one who created the stars and paints every sunset. Rest your head against His chest. Tell Him your secrets, your hopes, your dreams, your fears. The closer you draw to His side, the more aware of God's constant presence you'll become.

Precious Child,

I understand your desire to have walked the earth when My Son did, but actually what you have is far better. Not only is He with you always—surrounding you with My presence—He now lives in you. It is in Him that you now live, move, and have your being. Just as Jesus promised, we will never leave you or forsake you. We are in you, around you, and we flow through you to bless others.

Spiritual things are not naturally discerned, but you can train your spirit to sense and recognize My presence more consistently. It is every bit as real as the furniture you are sitting on—only My presence is eternal and it brings hope, health, peace, joy, and contentment.

Your loving Father

God's Will

We have not ceased praying for you and asking that you may
be filled with the knowledge of God's will in all spiritual
wisdom and understanding.

COLOSSIANS 1:9 NRSV

Do not conform any longer to the pattern of this world,
but be transformed by the renewing of your mind.
Then you will be able to test and approve what God's will is—
his good, pleasing and perfect will.

ROMANS 12:2

Be joyful always; pray continually; give thanks in all circumstances, for this is God's will for you in Christ Jesus.

1 THESSALONIANS 5:16-18

Jesus said, "The sheep hear [a shepherd's] voice and come to
him; and he calls his own sheep by name and leads them out.
He walks ahead of them; and they follow him,
for they recognize his voice. . . . I am the Good Shepherd."

JOHN 10:3-4,11 TLB

The [Holy] Spirit . . . pleads for us in harmony
with God's own will.

ROMANS 8:27 TLB

THE TREASURE INSIDE

Geocaching is a great way to spend an afternoon. With the help of a handheld GPS (Global Positioning System), directional coordinates from a geocache Internet site, and the desire for a little adventure, you can take part in a high-tech treasure hunt. Utilizing both your GPS and your brain to unravel clues and coordinates, you'll be led to a carefully concealed cache of inexpensive trinkets. The rule is "take one, leave one." But the knickknack you take home isn't the true treasure. It's the fun, challenge, and camaraderie you share with friends along the way that's truly valuable.

Some people regard God's will as a kind of geocache adventure. They feel if they have the right coordinates and take all the right turns, they will end up at just the right place—and wind up securing God's greatest treasure for their lives. The problem with this view is that if you make one wrong choice, you could miss a crucial turn and wind up miles away from that "one spot" God has set aside for you.

Your Father is a God of second chances. He promises that when you follow Him, He will bring good out of every circumstance, even if you've taken a wrong turn. God's Spirit and His Word are the ultimate GPS. As you rely on them day by day, you will find the wisdom you need to go the direction that best honors Him.

While God cares about the direction you're going, His primary concern is who you are becoming. In Scripture, God clearly says that His will for your life is for your heart to conform to the character of His own. What greater treasure could there be?

God's Word

Your word is a lamp for my feet
and a light for my path.
PSALM 119:105 NLT

Your words are what sustain me; they are food to my hungry
soul. They bring joy to my sorrowing heart and delight me.
JEREMIAH 15:16 TLB

The Word that God speaks is alive and full of power [making
it active, operative, energizing, and effective]; it is sharper
than any two-edged sword, penetrating to the dividing line of
the breath of life . . . and . . . spirit, and . . . [of the deepest
parts of our nature], exposing and sifting and analyzing and
judging the very thoughts and purposes of the heart.
HEBREWS 4:12 AMP

The Lord said, "This book of the law shall not depart from
your mouth, but you shall meditate on it day and night, so
that you may be careful to do according to all that is written in
it; for then you will make your way prosperous, and then you
will have success."
JOSHUA 1:8 NASB

THE WELL-TRAVELED WOMAN

You are a prepared woman. Before you head out on a road trip, you make sure you have a reliable car, bottled water, tools to change a tire, a full tank of gas, and an accurate map. However, having a map in your glove compartment can't help you find your way unless you use it. Similarly, having a Bible on your shelf won't make any difference in your life unless you read it and take its message to heart.

God's Word is more than just another book on the shelf. It's a Road Map for life. Unlike a regular map that contains street names and mileage markers, this Map is written in love letters, history lessons, prophecies, proverbs, biographies, poetry—even postcards from the borders of heaven that sometimes sound like science fiction. But there is a thread of truth running through it all—truth that remains steadfast throughout centuries, millenniums, and eternity itself. This truth helps provide you with what you need to know to navigate your way through time toward heaven.

In your life, every day is unexplored territory. It's easy to get lost or sidetracked along the way. The better acquainted you are with God's Road Map, the more you'll begin to notice something familiar in unfamiliar, or even hostile, territory. You'll begin to see and know God's hand at work. Reading a few verses or chapters of the Bible each day and asking God to use what you've read to make your heart more like His may not change the circumstantial landscape of your life. But it will change you, the intrepid—and dearly loved—traveler. It will make you more than a prepared woman. It will transform you into a purpose-driven, heaven-blessed, joy-filled daughter of God.

Grace

The amazing grace of the Master, Jesus Christ,
the extravagant love of God, the intimate friendship of the Holy
Spirit, be with all of you.

2 CORINTHIANS 13:14 MSG

If your life honors the name of Jesus, he will honor you.
Grace is behind and through all of this, our God giving himself
freely, the Master, Jesus Christ, giving himself freely.

2 THESSALONIANS 1:12 MSG

Now God has us where he wants us, with all the time in this world
and the next to shower grace and kindness upon us in Christ Jesus.

EPHESIANS 2:7 MSG

Even though on the outside it often looks like things are falling
apart on us, on the inside, where God is making new life,
not a day goes by without his unfolding grace.

2 CORINTHIANS 4:16 MSG

From his fullness we have all received, grace upon grace.
The law indeed was given through Moses; grace and
truth came through Jesus Christ.

JOHN 1:16-17 NRSV

Heavenly Father,

The whole concept of grace is hard for me to comprehend. I grew up hearing things like "Money doesn't grow on trees," "You get what you pay for," and "There are no free lunches." What a radical departure from this mind-set is Your boundless grace!

Why is that so difficult for me to accept? I always feel as if I should do something to be more deserving of this gift. And since I realize there is nothing I could ever do to earn it, I often feel unworthy.

I may never totally grasp the enormity of grace, but I ask You to help me grow in my understanding of it and to help me learn to apply it in my life. With Your help, Father, I receive Your amazing grace today.

Amen.

ERASED FOR ETERNITY

Bette Nesmith Graham was an erratic typist. She was also a budding artist. Frustrated by the smudges she caused trying to erase her typing errors, Bette leaned on her painting expertise for help. She mixed a batch of white paint to match the color of her typing paper. The next morning, Bette took a small bottle of the paint and a tiny brush with her to work, prepared to face the inevitable typos.

Bette's bottle of "Mistake Out" was the hit of the office. Every secretary wanted to have a bottle of her very own. In 1956, Bette started the Mistake Out Company, mixing up bottles of paint in her home. Soon after, she changed the name of her invention to Liquid Paper. In 1979, Bette sold her company to Gillette for $47 million. With the profits, she set up two charitable foundations for women. Bette made millions on the fact that everyone makes mistakes.[6]

Recall some of the mistakes you've made in your life—ones that are more serious than typos. Don't you wish you could simply make them disappear with a little Mistake Out? God has given you a better and more permanent way to do exactly that. When you ask God for forgiveness, He answers with a shower of grace. Grace doesn't just excuse or cover up the errors of your life; it erases them completely. It makes your heart as clean and spotless as a fresh piece of typing paper. And God's gift of grace is available to you for free because Jesus already paid for it with His death on the cross. So the next time you blow it, remember God's grace is just a prayer away.

Precious Child,

The beauty of grace is that you don't have to do anything but receive it. That's what grace is all about—favor from Me that is totally unmerited. You're right, there is nothing you could possibly do to earn or deserve My grace, but that's the point. It is a free gift, available to anyone who will receive it.

Your entrance into heaven is made possible by grace, but grace is not limited to paying your heavenly "fare." It provides moment-by-moment assistance to help you deal with all the challenges and stresses of your earthly life now. When your effort to overcome sin and bad habits is beyond your own ability, My grace enables you to triumph. When you blow it and need forgiveness, it is My grace that wipes the slate clean. In short, My grace is sufficient for your every need.

Your loving Father

Grief

The LORD is close to the brokenhearted
and saves those who are crushed in spirit.
PSALM 34:18

Surely He has borne our griefs
And carried our sorrows; . . .
And by His stripes we are healed.
ISAIAH 53:4-5 NKJV

Jesus said, "Very truly, I tell you, you will weep and mourn,
but the world will rejoice; you will have pain,
but your pain will turn into joy."
JOHN 16:20 NRSV

He will not break the bruised reed, nor quench the
dimly burning flame. He will encourage the fainthearted,
those tempted to despair.
ISAIAH 42:3 TLB

Jesus said, "Blessed are those who mourn,
For they shall be comforted."
MATTHEW 5:4 NKJV

AT THE CROSSROADS

They stand at the wind-whipped crossroads, their black shawls falling away from their faces to reveal two women wrapped tightly in grief and each other's embrace. One is young, too young to be mourning the loss of her husband—but that's where her life has led. The face of the other is weathered with age. While a widow never truly gets over the loss of her first love, it's the recent death of her two sons that has broken her heart anew.

Now, mother-in-law and daughter-in-law face losing each other. Unable to support one another financially, they know they should head separate ways. But their love for each other outweighs both their grief and fear of the future. Whatever may come, they will face it together. Hands clenched, hearts united, they cling to each other and to the promise that God will meet their needs, no matter how deep the wounds in their hearts or how difficult the road ahead seems to be.

Grief is never easy. It's a road where you must choose your traveling companions wisely. Just don't travel it alone. Lean on God and those you love when your heart is broken. Let tears be your prayer when words fail. Ask for help when you need it. Accept it wholeheartedly when it's offered.

The road ahead is leading you toward a new horizon, unfamiliar, yet not without promise. Just look at Ruth and Naomi: God led them from grief to a new life and a new love that allowed them to become part of the lineage of Jesus. Your journey toward healing has been charted with just as much care.

Guidance

Let the peace (soul harmony which comes) from Christ rule (act as umpire continually) in your hearts [deciding and settling with finality all questions that arise in your minds].
COLOSSIANS 3:15 AMP

You will hear a voice say, "This is the way;
turn around and walk here."
ISAIAH 30:21 NLT

The LORD says, "I will make you wise and show you where to go. I will guide you and watch over you."
PSALM 32:8 NCV

 This God is our God for ever and ever;
he will be our guide even to the end.
PSALM 48:14

The LORD of hosts . . .
Is wonderful in counsel and excellent in guidance.
ISAIAH 28:29 NKJV

Follow GOD'S example in everything you do.
EPHESIANS 5:1 TLB

STAYING IN STEP WITH GOD

If you're a woman who is daring enough to venture into a ballroom dance studio, one of the first lessons you'll learn is that, when it comes to the dance floor, guys get to lead. Your job is to follow. This doesn't make either partner more important than the other. After all, it takes two to tango. But this arrangement adds grace, beauty, and joy to the dance itself, alleviating the fumbling, frustration, and bruised toes that often arise when both partners try to head in opposite directions.

When it comes to making your way across the dance floor of life, God is the ultimate Dance Partner. It only makes sense to let Him lead. While you're dancing backwards (and in heels), God can see straight ahead into the future. He will wisely lead you around obstacles and hold you firmly in His arms when the pace of life changes unexpectedly from a waltz to a polka. He will teach you steps you never thought you could master and will help you dance more beautifully than you ever could on your own.

The more you open your heart to the spiritual side of life, the easier it will be to hear God's heavenly music. As you catch the rhythm of real life through prayer, through the guidelines God has given you in the Bible, and through God's own Spirit tugging at your heartstrings, you will gain a clearer understanding of which direction God wants you to go.

In God's eyes, you're the belle of the ball. Enjoy the dance of life by placing yourself in His arms. The more you lean on Him, the easier it will be to follow His lead.

Guilt

I finally admitted all my sins to you and stopped trying to hide
them. I said to myself, "I will confess them to the Lord."
And you forgave me! All my guilt is gone.

PSALM 32:5 TLB

As far as the east is from the west,
so far has he removed our transgressions from us.

PSALM 103:12

What happiness for those whose guilt has been forgiven!
What joys when sins are covered over! What relief for those who
have confessed their sins and God has cleared their record.

PSALM 32:1-2 TLB

Keep me from deliberate sins!
Don't let them control me.
Then I will be free of guilt.

PSALM 19:13 NLT

Let us draw near to God with a sincere heart
in full assurance of faith, having our hearts sprinkled
to cleanse us from a guilty conscience.

HEBREWS 10:22

Heavenly Father,

Guilt is something I am far too familiar with. Not only have I allowed others to put me on guilt trips, I live with my own self-condemnation because of my many shortcomings and failures. It seems as though I never quite measure up to my own expectations and am left feeling unworthy of You and Your blessings. I can relate to Eeyore from the Winnie the Pooh series—a dark cloud hovering over me everywhere I go. Even when the sun is shining and he is surrounded by good things, Eeyore stays trapped in the prison of his own making.

I need help with this, Lord, because this guilt is robbing me of experiencing the joyful, abundant life that Jesus has provided, and I know that cannot please You.

Amen.

PREVENTING FALSE ALARMS

Guilt has a purpose. Like an internal warning system, it alerts you to the fact that you've breached enemy territory. Its message is simple. "You've done something wrong. Now, go make it right." When this warning system is working correctly, this message will replay until you've gone to God, owned up to what you've done, accepted His forgiveness, and made any amends that need to be made. At this point, God turns off the message and your conscience is once again clear. Guilt has done its job. It's helped reconcile your relationship with your heavenly Father.

At least that's the way it's supposed to work. But some people refuse to accept the fact that God's grace is big enough to really forgive whatever they've done. So they manually turn the warning system back on. They may have done this so many times that their actions feel automatic. They feel as though God is judging them when it's really the other way around. They are the ones who are judging themselves.

Let guilt do its job and God do His. When you go the wrong way, turn around. Head straight back into your Father's arms. Accept His unconditional forgiveness. You can mourn the bad choices you've made and feel remorse over how you've hurt someone who loves you so much. But once you've asked God for His forgiveness, rest assured it's yours. It's time to forgive yourself the way God has forgiven you—once and for all.

Precious Child,

It hurts My heart to see you burdened with guilt, because it prevents you from experiencing My joy.

Guilt has its place, however. It is to your spirit what fever is to your body. One of the first indicators that your body is sick is that your temperature rises. Likewise, when you sin, guilt indicates that something is amiss.

The good news is, just as fever leaves the body when it is well, guilt is washed away by the blood of Jesus. When you confess your sin, I immediately cleanse you from it. Then I forget it. I want you to forget it too. It won't be easy because your enemy will try to replay the issue over and over again. But if you will discipline your mind to think on the truth of My Word, you can come out of the fog of guilt and dance in the sunshine.

Your loving Father

Health

They cried to the Lord in their trouble,
and he saved them from their distress;
he sent out his word and healed them.
PSALM 107:19-20 NRSV

I am the LORD who heals you.
EXODUS 15:26 NLT

You shall serve the LORD your God, and He will bless
your bread and your water. And I will take sickness
away from the midst of you.
EXODUS 23:25 NKJV

GOD blesses those who are kind to the poor.
. . . He nurses them when they are sick,
and soothes their pains and worries.
PSALM 41:1,3 TLB

He was wounded for our transgressions, he was bruised for
our iniquities: the chastisement of our peace was upon him;
and with his stripes we are healed.
ISAIAH 53:5 KJV

THE HEALING TOUCH

The crowd surges like a human wave—pushing steadily forward, straining to get close to Jesus, the famous One. Amid the sea of desperate fingers longing to touch Him, one frail hand grasps the back of His robe for a brief second before being pulled away by the push of the crowd (Luke 8:43-47). Jesus stops, turning to look at the tide of humanity pressing against Him. "Who touched Me?" He asks.

For a moment, there's silence. It seems a ridiculous question. Jesus is surrounded by the hands of the needy—those who are sick in body or spirit—those who need healing, comfort, and hope. But there is one woman who knows Jesus' question is directed at her. She tries to meet His eyes with her own, but she can't see through her tears. For twelve years she's suffered, going from doctor to doctor for answers, spending every last coin in search of relief. Now here she stands, whole and healed—all because of a single touch.

Now it's Jesus' turn to reach out to touch her. He tenderly lifts the woman's chin so she can look straight into His eyes. "Your faith has healed you," Jesus says with a smile. In that moment, the woman knows her life will never be the same again.

Your health and your wholeness matter to God. Reach out to touch Him in prayer. Bring both your pain and your praises. You will be transformed as you receive the gift of His life-changing touch.

Holy Spirit

We have not received the spirit of the world but the Spirit who is from God, that we may understand what God has freely given us. . . . We speak, not in words taught us by human wisdom but in words taught by the Spirit, expressing spiritual truths in spiritual words.

1 CORINTHIANS 2:12-13

Jesus said, "When the Father sends the Counselor as my representative—and by the Counselor I mean the Holy Spirit—he will teach you everything and will remind you of everything I myself have told you."

JOHN 14:26 NLT

Jesus said, "I will send you the Comforter—the Holy Spirit, the source of all truth. He will come to you from the Father and will tell you all about me."

JOHN 15:26 TLB

Jesus said, "I will ask the Father, and he will give you another Counselor, who will never leave you. He is the Holy Spirit, who leads into all truth."

JOHN 14:16-17 NLT

I keep asking that the God of our LORD Jesus Christ . . . may give you the Spirit of wisdom and revelation, so that you may know him better.

EPHESIANS 1:17

SIGNS OF LIFE

The brush of a breeze against your face, the smell of lilacs after a gentle spring rain, a sunset cacophony of cicadas resounding through the trees—you don't have to actually see the wind, touch the flowers, or step on a bug to know they're real, to know they're close to you as an intricate part of your world and experience. You learn to discern their presence in other ways.

The same is true of God. You cannot see Him in a physical form, hear His voice as you would a friend's, or feel the touch of His arms as He enfolds you with comfort when you need it most. But through the gift of God's Spirit, you can discern God's presence and power. You can experience what it's like to be loved completely, for who you really are. You can know which way God wants you to go.

God's Spirit is your living, breathing Road Map for life. He nudges your conscience to help you stay on the right path. He tugs at your heart to reach out to those in need. He whispers words of hope and healing when you feel as though you've lost your way. He opens your mind to help you understand and apply what you read in His Word. He even takes your moans and sighs and translates them into the heavenly language of prayer.

Be alert for signs of God's Spirit in your life. He's there, close by, guiding you every step of the way.

Hope

The hope of the righteous ends in gladness.

PROVERBS 10:28 RSV

The LORD is good to those whose hope is in him,
to the one who seeks him.

LAMENTATIONS 3:25

May the God of hope fill you with all joy and peace in believing, so
that by the power of the Holy Spirit you may abound in hope.

ROMANS 15:13 RSV

The LORD looks after those who fear him,
those who put their hope in his love.
He saves them from death
and spares their lives in times of hunger.

PSALM 33:18-19 NCV

Against all hope, Abraham in hope believed and so became the
father of many nations, just as it had been said to him, "So shall
your offspring be."

ROMANS 4:18

Heavenly Father,

I just want to thank You for bringing hope to my life. When the bills come pouring in but the money doesn't, when my body isn't working as it should but the doctor can't seem to find anything wrong, when all the sundry storms of life blow me around, I find hope in the fact that we are family—You and I. That relationship gives me something to hang on to during the hard times.

Thank You, Lord, that I have hope regarding my future in this earthly life—a future that is greater and more wonderful than I could ever imagine. And thank You for the hope I have of dwelling with You forever in Your heavenly kingdom—all my troubles gone for good. Oh, what a day that will be!

Amen.

✦

HOPE FLOATS

The tiny reed basket catches a gentle current and begins floating downstream. All too soon, it's out of reach of the mother's still-open arms. "See where it goes," Jochebed whispers, turning away from her young daughter before her own heart forces her into the water to rescue the son she's hidden so carefully for the last three months.

Miriam is old enough to understand the danger but still young enough to find reason to skip among the reeds on the river's edge. She watches the basket drift and twirl, dancing on the water like a fragile, fallen leaf. Caught on a rock by the river's edge, the basket comes to a sudden stop. A baby's cry rises above the music of the dancing water. Miriam holds her breath as a beautiful young woman stops to listen. As Miriam tiptoes closer, she recognizes the daughter of Pharaoh now cradling her baby brother in her graceful arms.

When hope is placed in the care of an almighty God, miracles happen. Not only did Moses survive the order of death at Pharaoh's hand, but he wound up in Pharaoh's daughter's arms. Jochebed was paid to care for her own son (Ex. 2:3-10). Miriam lived to see Israel's hope of freedom at another miraculous shore as she watched God part the waters of the Red Sea through her younger brother's hand (Ex. 14:21-22).

Hold on to hope by holding tightly to God. Share your deepest desires and greatest fears with Him. Do what God asks you to do. Then, keep your eyes open. God still works wonders.

My Precious Child,

It's true! One day you will dwell in the mansion I've prepared for you. Every need will be met. Your body will no longer experience the ravages of age and illness. It will be perfect and whole. All will be well with you when you come to dwell with Me in My heavenly kingdom. You are right to place your hope in that.

It is also true that your hope should not be confined to someday in the future. I am also the God of the now. I am here to meet your need—now! I am here to touch and heal your body—now! I am here for you in trouble—now! Call on Me and place your hope in My faithfulness both now and in the future.

Your loving Father

Humility

Humble yourselves before the Lord and he will exalt you.

JAMES 4:10 RSV

I say, through the grace given unto me, to every man that is among you, not to think of himself more highly than he ought to think; but to think soberly, according as God hath dealt to every man the measure of faith.

ROMANS 12:3 KJV

All of you serve each other with humble spirits, for God gives special blessings to those who are humble, but sets himself against those who are proud. If you will humble yourselves under the mighty hand of God, in his good time he will lift you up.

1 PETER 5:5-6 TLB

Toward the scorners he is scornful, but to the humble he shows favor.

PROVERBS 3:34 NRSV

All who humble themselves before the Lord shall be given every blessing, and shall have wonderful peace.

PSALM 37:11 TLB

AN ACCURATE IMAGE

You were created from the dust of the earth and the breath of God. Your human frame is fragile, finite, and prone to weakness. At the same time, you are precious, priceless, eternal, and pure. God fashioned you with His own hands, knitting you together in His own image. You are both wholly unique and yet one of countless generations. You are a sinner and a saint—a woman marred by disobedience and made whole by forgiveness, a prodigal child who has returned to a waiting Father, a priestess who has been declared holy so she can stand in the presence of a perfect God.

Humility begins with knowing who you are. It is not thinking less of yourself than God does. It is seeing yourself clearly through His eyes. Because Jesus knew exactly who He was—that He was God. He had every reason to be prideful. After all, no one else could compare to Him. Yet He chose to humble Himself, taking on a servant's role in washing His disciples' feet (John 13:12)—allowing Himself to die a criminal's death out of His love for you.

If you want to see what humility looks like in real life, look at Jesus. Then, look back at yourself. Having a clear picture of who you are—and who He is—will help you keep pride or a poor self-image in check.

Identity

You are a chosen people, a royal priesthood, a holy nation, a people belonging to God, that you may declare the praises of him who called you out of darkness into his wonderful light.

1 PETER 2:9

Jesus said, "You didn't choose me! I chose you! I appointed you to go and produce lovely fruit always."

JOHN 15:16 TLB

Jesus said, "You are the light that gives light to the world. . . . Live so that they will see the good things you do and will praise your Father in heaven."

MATTHEW 5:14,16 NCV

You are a people set apart as holy to GOD, your God. GOD, your God, chose you out of all the people on Earth for himself as a cherished, personal treasure.

DEUTERONOMY 7:6 MSG

The apostle Paul said, "I have been crucified with Christ; and it is no longer I who live, but Christ lives in me; and the life which I now live in the flesh I live by faith in the Son of God, who loved me and gave Himself up for me."

GALATIANS 2:20 NASB

THE REAL YOU

Identity theft is big news. You can take every precaution by shredding documents that contain your personal information and vigilantly guarding your social security and credit card numbers—but you can still become a victim. All you can really do about this problem is act wisely and leave the future in God's able hands.

But there's another type of identity "theft" that can be even more destructive. And it's one you can easily prevent. You can avert it by knowing, and remembering, who you really are. If God gave you an identity card, it would state that you are His beloved daughter forever and always. Instead of height and weight, it would list all of the amazing things God has woven into your character. Under your permanent address, it would read *heaven* because your name has been written in indelible ink in the Book of Life.

Even though this card is imaginary, the truth it contains is real. It's as permanent as God himself. But all too often, God's own children carry around counterfeit identity cards engraved on their hearts by past hurts, self-doubt, and the fear of failure. The information on these cards can include words such as *ordinary, unlovable, stupid, abandoned, worthless, alone.*

If you've been carrying a card such as this around, shred it. Use God's truth to rip apart every falsehood you have ever believed about who you are. Don't let lies steal your identity. Let God's truth set you free to dance and sing and laugh and create and love and be yourself in the fullest sense of the word. You are a woman of beauty and worth—a daughter of the King. Hold tightly to that truth.

Integrity

The LORD does not look at the things man looks at. Man looks at
the outward appearance, but the LORD looks at the heart.

1 SAMUEL 16:7

I will be careful to live a blameless life—
. . . I will lead a life of integrity
in my own home.

PSALM 101:2 NLT

Happy are people of integrity,
who follow the law of the LORD.

PSALM 119:1 NLT

You are to live clean, innocent lives as children of God in
a dark world full of people who are crooked and stubborn.
Shine out among them like beacon lights, holding out
to them the Word of Life.

PHILIPPIANS 2:15-16 TLB

You have upheld me because of my integrity,
and set me in your presence forever.

PSALM 41:12 NRSV

Heavenly Father,

The desire of my heart is to be a person of integrity—a person whom others can trust and a person whom You can trust. I want to be the same all the time regardless of who is watching or not watching. I don't want my life to be a "performance" in which I can never relax and be true to who I am, true to the person You've created me to be.

When I mess up, Father, give me the courage to take responsibility for my actions. When I'm tempted to tell half-truths, give me wise words and the boldness to speak the truth in love. And when fear tries to make me shrink back, give me the fortitude to be real—a true person of integrity who reflects Your nature.

Amen.

VIRTUOUS OR VIRTUAL?

Virtual reality is part of your daily life. You can speak to a girlfriend on your cell phone and carry on a conversation just as if she were actually there with you. You can see a virtual picture of yourself at your favorite salon that will give you an idea of what you would look like with a different hairstyle. You can even have a virtual office, with a receptionist who answers all of your business calls and forwards them to where you really work—the kitchen table of your apartment.

Virtual reality can be useful, but it is virtual. You are not "with" your girlfriend, you don't have the head of hair you see, and you don't really work at an office—just a filing cabinet and laptop crammed into your breakfast nook.

When it comes to integrity, you can choose to walk around with virtual morality. You can do all the right things when you're out in public where others can see you. But unless integrity is a reality in your heart, what you do will be an act, a virtual picture of what you wish you looked like but haven't allowed God to actually develop in your character.

Do something countercultural. Be authentic. Be real—inside and out. Even if you make mistakes or poor choices, own up to them—to yourself, to others, and to God. Allow God to soften your pride and toughen your resolve. As you grow to more resemble Him, you'll find you have the strength and desire to do only what you know God would be proud of—regardless of whether anyone else is watching or not.

My Precious Child,

It blesses My heart to hear of your desire to be authentic in a world filled with deception and game playing. Integrity is so rare that it is one of the most effective ways that you can testify of the difference Christ has made in your life. When you are real, great light shines forth from you that cuts through the darkness that is so pervasive in the world.

I took great care in creating you, and only when you are true to your heart can you fulfill the destiny I've planned for your life. Don't cheat the people with whom you come into contact by settling for a cheap imitation. Be the real deal. When you are, your life reflects My heart—My integrity—to the world.

Your loving Father

Jesus Christ

Now we rejoice in our wonderful new relationship with God—
all because of what our Lord Jesus Christ has done in dying
for our sins—making us friends of God.
ROMANS 5:11 TLB

The Son is the radiance of God's glory and
the exact representation of his being.
HEBREWS 1:3

Jesus said, "I am the good shepherd; I know my own sheep,
and they know me, just as my Father knows me and I know the
Father. And I lay down my life for the sheep."
JOHN 10:14-15 NLT

Jesus said, "I am the Light of the world; he who follows Me
will not walk in the darkness, but will have the Light of life."
JOHN 8:12 NASB

Jesus Christ is the same yesterday and today and for ever.
HEBREWS 13:8 RSV

Jesus said, "Take My yoke upon you and learn from Me,
for I am gentle and lowly in heart, and you will find
rest for your souls."
MATTHEW 11:29 NKJV

RELATIONSHIP PAINTS A PICTURE

When your mind paints a picture of Jesus, what does it look like? Does it flash back to paintings you've seen of Him enjoying a group of children or praying in the Garden of Gethsemane? Does it incorporate stories you've read from the Bible where you can visualize Jesus' anger with the Pharisees, His agony on the cross, or His compassion for those who are suffering? Whether your picture is a composite of artwork, Scripture, or the opinions of others, your image will be incomplete until the day you meet Jesus face-to-face. But don't let that stop you from trying to catch a glimpse of Him each and every day.

Getting a clear picture of someone the Bible describes as both fully God and fully human can be quite a challenge. There's so much to take in. In the same way that a little child can't grasp the concepts of calculus, your brain cannot fully understand the depth and breadth of Jesus and His love for you. However, a child can begin to understand numbers—the building blocks of calculus. Grasping one building block at a time in regard to Jesus will take you one step closer to seeing Him more clearly.

Take hold of how Jesus describes Himself in Scripture. Consider how you've experienced His power in your life. Ask Him to reveal Himself in ways that will help you paint a more accurate picture of Him in your mind and heart. The better you get to know Him, the more you'll be able to see how His image is becoming more apparent in you.

Joy

If we are living in the light of God's presence,
just as Christ does, then we have wonderful fellowship and
joy with each other.
1 JOHN 1:7 TLB

You have endowed him with eternal happiness.
You have given him the unquenchable joy of your presence.
PSALM 21:6 TLB

Jesus said, "If you obey my commands, you will remain in my
love. I have told you these things so that you can have the same
joy I have and so that your joy will be the fullest possible joy."
JOHN 15:10-11 NCV

You have not seen Christ, but still you love him. You cannot
see him now, but you believe in him. So you are filled with a
joy that cannot be explained, a joy full of glory.
1 PETER 1:8 NCV

Salvation comes from God.
What joys he gives to all his people.
PSALM 3:8 TLB

ARE YOU IN YOUR SKIN?

"Jam bah doo nah?" If you were living in the African country of Cameroon, that's how you would greet your friends and family. You'd raise your hands open-palmed and hold them up in front of your chest as you asked, "Are you in your skin?" or, translated another way, "Is your soul in your body?"—to which the other person would wholeheartedly reply, "Yes, oh yes, I am alive!"

Is your soul in your body? Are you fully alive, both body and spirit? Living the abundant, joy-filled life God desires for you goes far beyond simply breathing in and out. It means keeping your soul awake and alert, watching for signs of God's presence and purpose in even the smallest details of your day. It means openly rejoicing with those who rejoice and weeping with those who weep. It means celebrating who you are and where you are at this moment, even when your day is far from what you would label as "perfect." It means walking through life hand in hand with God.

Authentic, heart-pumping, soul-satisfying joy is something that grows from the inside out. It's not dependent on the circumstances that surround you—on what you own, who you're with, or how successful your career happens to be. It springs up from the over-flow of a heart filled with God's goodness and grace. At times, it may feel a lot like happiness, except that it doesn't ebb and flow with your mood. Joy comes from being "in your skin," from being the real you, inside and out—fully present in the moment and trustingly committed to the One who cares so deeply for you, body and soul.

Love

This is how we know what real love is: Jesus gave his life for us. So we should give our lives for our brothers and sisters.

1 JOHN 3:16 NCV

Now that you have purified yourselves by obeying the truth so that you have sincere love for your brothers, love one another deeply, from the heart.

1 PETER 1:22

Love endures long and is patient and kind; love never is envious nor boils over with jealousy, is not boastful or vainglorious, does not display itself haughtily. It is not conceited (arrogant and inflated with pride); it is not rude (unmannerly) and does not act unbecomingly. Love (God's love in us) does not insist on its own rights or its own way, for it is not self-seeking; it is not touchy or fretful or resentful; it takes no account of the evil done to it [it pays no attention to a suffered wrong]. It does not rejoice at injustice and unrighteousness, but rejoices when right and truth prevail. Love bears up under anything and everything that comes, is ever ready to believe the best of every person, its hopes are fadeless under all circumstances, and it endures everything [without weakening]. Love never fails [never fades out or becomes obsolete or comes to an end].

1 CORINTHIANS 13:4-8 AMP

Heavenly Father,

No matter how hard I try, I just can't seem to love some people—especially the ones who get on my nerves or are very different from me. Then there are those who have hurt me. I've tried to forgive them, but I can't seem to pull it off. I know You command me to love even my enemies, but is that really possible? Sometimes I want to love people but the negative feelings are still churning inside. Then I feel like a phony, that I'm deceiving myself and them—it's just an act. That can't be pleasing to You.

I need Your help, Lord. Teach me to love as You love—from the heart. Point out to me the obstacles I've placed in the way of true, genuine love for people. I'm sure there must be something that I'm not seeing because Your Word says that true love never fails. I open myself to You. Show me how to love in deed and in truth.

Amen.

LOVE IN ACTION

The woman watches her feet slowly making their way over the dust-choked path leading outside the city gates. She dares not lift her tear-filled eyes from the ground for fear she will catch sight of her son's lifeless body and again be reduced to wracking sobs. She finds it hard to believe she's still moving at all—that her own heart is still beating under the weight of her grief. First her husband, now her son—gone. Never again will she know the comfort of real family. Never again will she know the joy of being loved purely and unconditionally.

From the corner of her eye, she sees another set of feet join the rhythm of her own—sandaled, masculine, equally dusty. A man's voice, tender yet undergirded with strength, whispers, "Don't cry." The widow can't help but look up. Her eyes meet the Stranger's for a moment. In that brief time, she's overcome with the feeling that the depth of love she's experienced thus far is just a taste of what lies ahead. The next words the Stranger speaks are to her dead son, who immediately responds to the man's bidding and gets up off his funerary pallet to comfort his mother, whose tears change in an instant from grief to awe to unbridled joy.

Jesus' love led Him to bring a grieving widow's son back to life. The woman didn't seek Jesus out or plead for a miracle. But Jesus knew what was behind her tears—and He couldn't pass by without reaching out in compassion. Follow Jesus' example. Put yourself in the shoes of those in need. Then, allow love to work wonders through you.

My Precious Child,

You're right to think that love is something you can't fake. You know it isn't real, and the other person can see through your flimsy deception as well. It's time to face the fact that there are just some people you will never be able to love—on your own, that is. Even when you try to clothe yourself with love, sometimes you have to grow into the clothes. Still, you do have options.

When you find yourself in a situation where your love—however well intentioned—falls short of the mark, ask Me to love that person through you. Make yourself a channel for My strong, supernatural, eternal love to flow through you to the person in question. Do that long enough, and you will find your own ability to love deepened and purified.

Your loving Father

Ministry

Jesus said, "You did not choose Me but I chose you,
and appointed you that you would go and bear fruit,
and that your fruit would remain."

JOHN 15:16 NASB

Just as our bodies have many parts and each part has a special
function, so it is with Christ's body. We are all parts of his one
body, and each of us has different work to do. And since we
are all one body in Christ, we belong to each other, and each
of us needs all the others. God has given each of us the ability
to do certain things well.

ROMANS 12:4-6 NLT

There are different kinds of spiritual gifts, but it is the same
Holy Spirit who is the source of them all. There are different
kinds of service in the church, but it is the same Lord we are
serving. There are different ways God works in our lives,
but it is the same God who does the work through all of us.
A spiritual gift is given to each of us as a means of helping the
entire church. . . . It is the one and only Holy Spirit who
distributes these gifts. He alone decides which gift
each person should have.

1 CORINTHIANS 12:4-7,11 NLT

We are his workmanship, created in Christ Jesus
for good works, which God prepared beforehand,
that we should walk in them.

EPHESIANS 2:10 RSV

YOUR IMPACT ON THE WORLD

You are a priestess. That may sound a little daunting. It may even sound like something you have no desire to be. But the Bible says that once you choose to follow God instead of choosing to run the other way, you instantly become part of a prestigious and everlasting priesthood—along with the likes of leaders such as Peter, Paul, Abraham, and Moses.

There are a lot of men's names in the Bible, but that doesn't exclude all of the women who worked hand in hand with God to accomplish great things throughout history—women such as Sarah, Rahab, and Esther. God invites you to be one of these women—to help others see God more clearly by allowing His power to work through you.

Your ministry is simply another name for the work that God equips and directs you to do. Sometimes it's within your church. Sometimes it's within your family. Sometimes it's in your neighborhood—or on the other side of the world. What you do and whom you minister to may change along with the seasons of your life. But wherever and whenever God leads you, whatever special place He has created for you to fill is not something to be afraid of. It's something to look forward to.

Before you were born, God wove into your character a unique combination of talents and gifts. Later, when you choose to put your life in God's hands, other spiritual gifts come to light. The true beauty of your gifts becomes evident only once they are given away. Give yourself away today by serving God and others. Your ministry matters in this world.

Nurturing

When my father and my mother forsake me,
Then the LORD will take care of me.
PSALM 27:10 NKJV

When they had eaten breakfast, Jesus said to Simon Peter,
"Simon, son of Jonah, do you love Me more than these?" He
said to Him, "Yes, Lord; You know that I love You," He said
to him, "Feed My lambs." He said to him again a second
time, "Simon, son of Jonah, do you love Me?" He said to
Him, "Yes, Lord; You know that I love You." He said to him,
"Tend My sheep." He said to him the third time, "Simon,
son of Jonah, do you love Me?" Peter was grieved because He
said to him the third time, "Do you love Me?" And he said to
Him, "Lord, You know all things. You know that I love You."
Jesus said to him, "Feed My sheep."
JOHN 21:15-17 NKJV

Encourage one another and build up one another,
just as you also are doing.
1 THESSALONIANS 5:11 NASB

He will feed his flock like a shepherd;
he will gather the lambs in his arms,
and carry them in his bosom.
ISAIAH 40:11 NRSV

NURTURERS NEED NURTURING TOO

The Bible is filled with pictures of God drawn with strokes of metaphor. He's a Rock, a Warrior, a strong Tower, a Father, a consuming Fire. While all of these snapshots give you a glimpse of the character of the Almighty, they are only part of the picture. God created both men's and women's hearts in His image. That means God also has a softer side. It's true He's a powerful protector, but He's also a tender nurturer. Like a gardener who delights in helping things grow, God provides what His children need to mature and thrive. He "mothers" them, as well as "fathers" them.

You don't have to have children to be a nurturer. Nurturing others is part of your spiritual DNA. Every time you offer tender care to those in need, mentor others on their own road to success, or simply long to "kiss and make it all better" in the lives of those who are closest to your heart, the nurturer in you rises to the surface. So does a beautiful reflection of God's image.

But sometimes being a nurturer can leave you feeling responsible for the progress of those you're choosing to come alongside to help, as though the problems or setbacks of those you're caring for are your own. Never forget, though you're working hand in hand with God to help another, every person's journey is ultimately between that individual and God alone. Your own growth and vitality is no less important than those you are nurturing.

So when you give of yourself, renew yourself with a little nurturing of your own. Take time to relax and reconnect with God. Allow others to care for you when you need it. It's a great way to keep going—and growing.

Obedience

What is more pleasing to the LORD: your burnt offerings
and sacrifices or your obedience to his voice? Obedience is far
better than sacrifice. Listening to him is much better
than offering the fat of rams.

1 SAMUEL 15:22 NLT

Jesus replied, "'Love the Lord your God with all your heart,
soul, and mind.' This is the first and greatest commandment.
The second most important is similar: 'Love your neighbor as
much as you love yourself.' All the other commandments and
all the demands of the prophets stem from these two laws and
are fulfilled if you obey them. Keep only these and you will find
that you are obeying all the others."

MATTHEW 22:37-40 TLB

The Lord says,
"If you are willing and obedient,
you will eat the best from the land."

ISAIAH 1:19

When we obey him, every path he guides us on is fragrant
with his lovingkindness and his truth.

PSALM 25:10 TLB

Heavenly Father,

I remember as a child thinking, *I can't wait to grow up and not have to follow all these rules. When I become a mom, I'm going to be nice and let my kids do whatever they want.*

Now that I'm an adult, I see how foolish that thinking was. The reality is that even though I don't have a parent telling me what to do, I still have to obey—the laws of the land, my boss, the laws of nature, and You. If I don't, there will be negative consequences.

When it comes to obeying You, sometimes I'm not sure what it is You want me to do. Then, I must be honest, sometimes I know the right thing to do, but I just don't want to do it—just like a little child. Forgive me for those times, Lord, and help me to be quick to obey You.

Amen.

CHOOSE YOUR SHOES WISELY

Step back in time for just a moment. Put yourself in the Mary Janes of childhood and recall some of the rules you were expected to follow each day: Do your homework. Don't snack between meals. When you use something, put it back where you found it. Look before you cross the street. Don't run with scissors. Wash behind your ears. Don't play with matches. Brush your teeth. Don't hit your sister, brother, dog, cat, fish, or friend—the list could go on and on.

As an adult, you understand that rules like these are born of love, not a desire for power or as an antidote to boredom. Parents want what's best for their kids. They want them to be safe, to mature, to live up to their potential, and to enjoy life. Your heavenly Father wants the same for you. That's why your obedience is so important to Him.

Every "thou shalt" and "thou shalt not" recorded in the Bible is there to point you in the direction of a better life, a godly life— one that honors God, yourself, and others. Sometimes your childish heart will feel the same way you did in those Mary Janes. Your rebellious spirit will feel that the rules are unfair, unnecessary, and a real bother when you have plans of your own that are pulling you in the opposite direction. When that happens, put on your grown-up shoes. Remember, God has your best interest in mind. His rules are not arbitrary decrees or old-fashioned edicts. Each is a love letter straight from His heart.

Precious Child,

Obedience is something all humans struggle with. Your fleshly nature wants to go its own way and do its own thing. But you're right: when you do that, there are always negative consequences.

It will help if you are fully persuaded of My good and loving nature. I have only your best interest in mind when I give you instructions to obey.

My Word is filled with examples of those who obeyed Me and those who didn't. It is true today—as it was then—that the willing and obedient are the ones who reap the blessings.

Another factor that you may not be aware of is that I will help you to obey Me. I am always at work in you, creating the power and desire to do My will. Be willing to be willing, and I will help you to obey.

Your loving Father

The Opposite Sex

In Christ Jesus you are all children of God through faith. . . .
There is no longer male and female; for all of you are
one in Christ Jesus.
GALATIANS 3:26,28 NRSV

God created man in His own image, in the image of God He
created him; male and female He created them.
GENESIS 1:27 NASB

The LORD God said, "It is not good that the man should be
alone; I will make him a helper fit for him." . . . So the LORD
God caused a deep sleep to fall upon the man, and while he
slept took one of his ribs and closed up its place with flesh;
and the rib which the LORD God had taken from the man he
made into a woman and brought her to the man. Then the
man said, "This at last is bone of my bones and flesh of my
flesh; she shall be called Woman,because she was
taken out of Man."
GENESIS 2:18,21-23 RSV

Out of respect for Christ,
be courteously reverent to one another.
EPHESIANS 5:21 MSG

THE BALANCE OF THE SEXES

When it comes to chromosomes, God gave some people two Xs and others a combination of Y and X. While God's original design was for men and women to complete each other—to present a more accurate reflection of His own image—men and women often compete against each other instead. One way they try to prove their own gender's value (or superiority) is by criticizing the opposite sex.

In God's eyes, men and women are equal in value. They are priceless creations. Does your view of the sexes reflect God's own?

In today's culture, male bashing is often considered entertainment. Whether it's a TV sitcom, a new joke on the Internet, or sharing husband stories with the girls, the invitation to join in the sport is all around you. You may even have some personal experiences with men in your life that you feel have given you valid reasons to put down the opposite sex.

But the truth is that every individual stands on his or her own when it comes to representing his or her own sex. Represent yours well by treating men and speaking about them with respect. If you have problems with a man in your life, first go to God for wisdom. Then meet with the individual to try and sort things out. Don't turn your personal struggles into generalizations about the male population. Enjoy the differences. Learn from them. Why not take a moment right now to thank God for them?

Patience

Better is the end of a thing than its beginning;
and the patient in spirit is better than the proud in spirit.
ECCLESIASTES 7:8 RSV

We can rejoice, too, when we run into problems and
trials for we know that they are good for us—they help us
learn to be patient. And patience develops
strength of character in us.
ROMANS 5:3-4 TLB

God will strengthen you with his own great power so that you
will not give up when troubles come, but you will be patient.
COLOSSIANS 1:11 NCV

Whatever things were written before were written for our
learning, that we through the patience and comfort of
the Scriptures might have hope.
ROMANS 15:4 NKJV

May the Lord lead your hearts into God's love
and Christ's patience.
2 THESSALONIANS 3:5 NCV

WATCHING AND WAITING

For months snow and ice have covered the ground. The soil lies hard and barren, void of any hint of life. But beneath the surface, God is at work. A crocus bulb is cracking, sprouting, sending delicate green shoots upward toward the light. One morning the newborn bud lifts its bowed head from the dark soil of winter into the dawn of day. Spring is finally on its way.

Every unique season of the year plays a vital role in how God's world functions. Bulbs need times of dormancy to prepare them for vibrant outbursts of growth. God has designed the timing of the seasons to coincide perfectly with their needs. He does the same with you. God knows when your development has reached a point where you can receive and enjoy what He has planned for you—be it a promotion, a cross-country move, a new relationship, or the answer to a prayer that has long been on your heart.

You can't hurry God and His timing any more than you can rush springtime. But you can choose to master the art of waiting as you reap the peace of a patient spirit. Patience grows right along with your trust in God. The more you trust God and His long track record of perfect timing, the easier it will be for you to watch and wait. Keep your eyes open for signs of change as eagerly as you would for the first buds of spring, announcing the imminent arrival of glorious things.

Peace

Don't worry about anything; instead, pray about everything;
tell God your needs and don't forget to thank him for his answers.
If you do this you will experience God's peace, which is far more
wonderful than the human mind can understand. His peace will
keep your thoughts and your hearts quiet and at rest as
you trust in Christ Jesus.

PHILIPPIANS 4:6-7 TLB

Jesus said, "I am leaving you with a gift—peace of mind and heart!
And the peace I give isn't fragile like the peace the world gives.
So don't be troubled or afraid."

JOHN 14:27 TLB

Following after the Holy Spirit leads to life and peace.

ROMANS 8:6 TLB

I will both lie down in peace, and sleep;
For You alone, O LORD, make me dwell in safety.

PSALM 4:8 NKJV

The LORD will give strength to His people;
The LORD will bless His people with peace.

PSALM 29:11 NKJV

Heavenly Father,

I really need Your peace. The circumstances of my life are closing in and threatening to overtake me. I face impossible situations; fear and stress have become my constant companions.

The news is filled with frightening images and scenarios. There are so many "what-ifs," most of which are beyond my control. Then there's the stress I deal with every day. It helps to make a to-do list, but as I race through my day to tackle each item, my body and my mind suffer from the tension. And even then I don't get everything done that I'd like.

Then I read about Your leading me beside still waters and restoring my soul. My spirit stirs within me. Could it be? Could I possibly enjoy that kind of peace?

I need Your help, Father. I just don't know how to let Your peace become my reality.

Amen.

THE PATH TO PEACE

People try an interesting variety of methods to achieve inner peace: Tai-chi, meditation, aromatherapy, self-help programs, walking labyrinths, visiting vortexes, burning empowering candles, cleansing their auras—or their colons. Even good old denial can promise to be a path to inner tranquility.

But there's only one path to an inner peace that can withstand outer turmoil. That path leads straight to God's presence. While "peace on Earth" sounds so promising on a Christmas card, Scripture says that there will always be war, natural disasters, poverty, and evil on this planet. At the same time, God promises to provide you with a peace that goes far beyond anything the world can offer. It's the peace that comes from putting your life in God's hands and knowing that together, you will do more than just make it through. You will know victory, joy, purpose, power, and eternal life firsthand.

Walking God's path to peace is a day-by-day process of learning to trust. Trusting that God is ultimately in control, that He is working behind the scenes to bring good out of every circumstance, that His plans for you are conceived out of bound-less wisdom and endless love, that your prayers are not only heard but answered, and that God's ways are perfect, and His Word is true—these are stepping-stones you must put your full weight on as you walk the path that leads you closer to Him.

On God's road map for life, the path of peace is clearly marked. When you're feeling anxious or worried, make sure your feet are set on the right road, leading straight into God's arms. Your peace will grow along with your trust in Him.

Dear Child,

Like Martha in the Bible, you are troubled about many things. It is Mary that I want you to emulate. Her life was filled with responsibilities and cares, too, but she knew the secret to peaceful living: she put first things first and sat at the Master's feet.

I know you are busy, but if you will seek Me early each day, I will help you set the pace and accomplish the truly necessary things. My yoke is easy and My burden is light, and that is how you can tell if your life is on track.

When impossible situations confront you, remember, all things are possible with Me. Embrace My promises and allow them to envelop your heart and mind. My Word and My presence will surround you with a "bubble" of peace, making you impervious to fear and stress. You have nothing to fear; I am here.

Your loving Father

Perseverance

Consider it all joy, my brethren, when you encounter various
trials, knowing that the testing of your faith produces
endurance. And let endurance have its perfect result, so that
you may be perfect and complete, lacking in nothing. . . .
Blessed is a man who perseveres under trial; for once he has
been approved, he will receive the crown of life which the
Lord has promised to those who love Him.

JAMES 1:2-4,12 NASB

You need to persevere so that when you have done the will of
God, you will receive what he has promised.

HEBREWS 10:36

In hope we have been saved, but hope that is seen is not hope;
for who hopes for what he already sees? But if we hope for
what we do not see, with perseverance we wait eagerly for it.

ROMANS 8:24-25 NASB

We consider blessed those who have persevered.
You have heard of Job's perseverance and have seen what
the Lord finally brought about. The Lord is full of
compassion and mercy.

JAMES 5:11

DON'T GIVE UP

There's an old joke former President Ronald Reagan used to tell about the effect a person's outlook has on his or her perseverance. He said when an optimistic person finds himself in manure he continues to dig because he knows there's a pony in there somewhere.

Some people are "pony seekers." They can keep moving forward when times are hard because they know God will bring something good out of every situation. Other people lean more toward being proverbial worrywarts. They focus on all of the bad things that could happen, even when life is going well. As a result, fear, doubt, procrastination, and negativity often keep these naysayers stuck in one place—or even push them backwards.

If you want to persevere—to maintain the energy and motivation it takes to keep moving forward when the headwinds of life are blowing in at hurricane strength—keep your eyes open for that pony. God weaves blessing into every day—even difficult ones. And as you persevere, if exhaustion or discouragement threatens to cloud your perspective, find some fellow pony seekers to help support and encourage you along the way. God will often allow situations into your life that are too big for you to handle on your own to help build a community of encouragers into your life.

Persevering through trials can teach you patience, make you stronger, and help you learn to lean on others when times are tough. But most of all, perseverance forces you to keep focused on God's eternal perspective. It reminds you that there's so much more treasure to be found in this life and the next than what can be seen with your eyes.

Power

I pray that you will begin to understand how incredibly great
his power is to help those who believe him. It is that same
mighty power that raised Christ from the dead.

EPHESIANS 1:19-20 TLB

I am not ashamed of the gospel,
for it is the power of God for salvation to
everyone who believes.

ROMANS 1:16 NASB

Jesus said, "When the Holy Spirit comes to you,
you will receive power."

ACTS 1:8 NCV

We have this treasure in earthen vessels, that the excellence of
the power may be of God and not of us.

2 CORINTHIANS 4:7 NKJV

My speech and my preaching were not with persuasive words
of human wisdom, but in demonstration of the Spirit and of
power, that your faith should not be in the wisdom of men
but in the power of God.

1 CORINTHIANS 2:4-5 NKJV

JUST PLUG IN

It's 110 degrees in the shade. After your second shower of the day, you're straining to hear the traffic report on the radio above the bellow of your blow dryer so you'll know when you need to leave to make it to the theater on time. Downstairs in the kitchen, the salmon you're broiling is almost ready, as is the load of laundry tumbling in the dryer. That's when the power blows.

A blackout can be a major inconvenience. But what happens when you have a blackout of a more personal nature? When life seems to be well under control, but then you're laid off at work, your daughter decides to drop out of high school, or the guy you thought was Mr. Right dumps you for someone new? It may be hard to accept, but feeling powerless can be good for you. That's because it forces you to face the fact that much of life is totally out of your control. It encourages you to seek a power source that is greater than your own.

The only Source of power that is strong enough to shape a galaxy, while gentle enough to heal a shattered heart, is God himself. When you connect your life with the God of the universe, you plug into a power Source that can never be cut off or run dry. Through prayer, you can tap into the power that held back the Red Sea (Ex. 14:21-22) and raised Lazarus from the dead (John 11:43-44). And as you get to know God better, you'll experience His power working through your own life, giving you the strength you need to face any circumstance that may come your way.

Prayer

God's Decree—
". . . They'll pray to me by name
and I'll answer them personally."
ZECHARIAH 13:8-9 MSG

Now this is the confidence that we have in Him, that if we ask
anything according to His will, He hears us. And if we know that
He hears us, whatever we ask, we know that we have the petitions
that we have asked of Him.
1 JOHN 5:14-15 NKJV

Jesus said, "Here's what I want you to do: Find a quiet,
secluded place so you won't be tempted to role-play before God.
Just be there as simply and honestly as you can manage.
The focus will shift from you to God, and you will begin to sense
his grace. The world is full of so-called prayer warriors who are
prayer—ignorant. They're full of formulas and programs and
advice, peddling techniques for getting what you want from God.
Don't fall for that nonsense. This is your Father you are dealing
with, and he knows better than you what you need. With a God like
this loving you, you can pray very simply."
MATTHEW 6:6-9 MSG

Why am I praying like this?
Because I know you will answer me, O God!
PSALM 17:6 TLB

Heavenly Father,

I've heard it said that prayer is simply conversation with You. Is that true? If so, maybe prayer is not as difficult as I have thought. Somehow I've had it in my mind that I had to pray certain words in a specific way in order to get through to You. I've pictured You to be like the Wizard of Oz—an ominous and mysterious being far beyond my grasp and too grand to be concerned with my silly cares. But when I read Your Word, a new picture is beginning to take shape.

Father, help me to see You as You really are— great and powerful, but at the same time gentle and easy to be entreated. I want to get to know You better.

Amen.

PORTRAIT OF PRAYER

Speaking to God should never be boring or tedious, even though at times prayer may feel like a one-sided conversation. When you call out to God, you are addressing the one and only Creator of the universe. Picture a small child trying to converse with an important head of state, and you get a very rough picture of what that exchange might look like. But God is greater than any leader and more powerful than any president. He is more intelligent than a Rhodes scholar and more compassionate than the mother of a newborn child. And He is always listening for your unique voice.

There are no magic words to pray. All God asks is that you be honest, open, and wholly present. Take time to confess your failings, express your concerns, and listen for God's direction. If you need a little help getting started, here are a few ways to talk to God you might want to try:

1. Write your own song of praise to God like those written in the book of Psalms. Read it or sing it aloud to Him.
2. Memorize a verse from the Bible that holds a special promise for your life. Close your eyes and mull those words over and over in your mind for several minutes. Ask God to help you gain new insight into what He wants you to learn.
3. Spend time thanking God for everything you can think of. Chances are, the time you have available will come to an end before your reasons for gratitude.
4. Ask God how you can love others more like He does. Just sit and listen. Then, act on what you hear.

Dear Child,

I am blessed by your desire to learn more about prayer. Yes, prayer is conversation with Me. And as is true for any true conversation, there is a protocol to be followed. First, each party must take turns speaking and listening. When you and I converse, I will listen as long as you want to pour out your heart, but then, don't forget that I have things to say as well.

Sometimes I will speak in the form of an impression you have in your heart. Other times I will lead you to certain scriptures to articulate the point I want to make. Try not to rush off before I've had a chance to finish, and try not to interrupt.

What I want to say is important and will impact your life in a positive and wonderful way. Keep a notebook handy, too, so you can write down the things we talk about.

Your loving Father

Priorities

Jesus said, "Seek first his kingdom and his righteousness, and all these things will be given to you as well."
MATTHEW 6:33

Jesus said, "You shall love the Lord your God with all your heart, and with all your soul, and with all your mind. This is the great and first commandment. And a second is like it, You shall love your neighbor as yourself."
MATTHEW 22:37-39 RSV

O GOD, You are my God;
Early will I seek You.
PSALM 63:1 NKJV

Remember to observe the Sabbath as a holy day. Six days a week are for your daily duties and your regular work, but the seventh day is a day of Sabbath rest before the Lord your God. On that day you are to do no work of any kind.
EXODUS 20:8-10 TLB

You chart the path ahead of me, and tell me where to stop and rest. Every moment, you know where I am.
PSALM 139:3 TLB

THE LAW OF LOVE

Dinner for sixteen! How do I get myself into situations like this? I know they've been traveling for a while, and I assumed they'd stay for dinner, but I didn't expect to have to prepare everything by myself. What's my sister doing? Nothing. Just sitting around while I do all the work. I've set the bread to rise and found enough clean plates to go around, but the meat and vegetables still have to be chopped for the stew and someone needs to make sure we have enough wine. Martha's thoughts bubble as vigorously as the stew will soon be cooking over the fire.

She walks into the main room where her guests are seated, her rapid gait broadcasting her growing frustration. Looking for apologies, help, and a bit of sympathy, Martha explains her dilemma to Jesus. To her surprise, Jesus shakes His head, softly chiding her worry and distraction while praising her sister's choice to simply sit at His feet, spending her limited time in His presence (Luke 10:38-42).

Knowing your priorities is important in determining how you'll spend the limited time you have each day, but that doesn't make choosing what to do next an exact science. Life is a juggling act where you need to learn to balance responsibilities, interruptions, desires, and opportunities. A key to keeping everything in balance is to keep Jesus' admonition to "love God and love people" always in mind. Ask God for wisdom when planning your day—and for the grace to know when to change your plans.

Purity

The LORD says,
"Come, let us talk about these things.
Though your sins are like scarlet,
they can be as white as snow.
Though your sins are deep red,
they can be white like wool."

ISAIAH 1:18 NCV

If we confess our sins, he is faithful and just and will forgive us
our sins and purify us from all unrighteousness.

1 JOHN 1:9

Purify me from my sins, and I will be clean;
wash me, and I will be whiter than snow.

PSALM 51:7 NLT

Jesus said,
"Blessed are the pure in heart,
for they will see God."

MATTHEW 5:8

To the pure you show yourself pure.

PSALM 18:26

IT ALL COMES OUT IN THE WASH

You don't have to work for CSI to unravel the mystery of pink underwear. When a load of whites comes out of the laundry with a rosy hue, you can be sure that despite your best sorting efforts, a renegade garment has made its way into the wrong load. The culprit is usually a red, noncolorfast item. All it takes is one tiny scarlet handkerchief to taint a whole load.

The same holds true when it comes to your own personal purity. Even one bad habit or dirty little secret takes its toll. That's the bad news. But the good news is, God promises you can once again be as pure as freshly driven snow—or as white as a load of newly bleached T-shirts. Through God's grace and forgiveness, you can live a pure and holy life even though it's an imperfect one.

Purity is not a prudish ideal. It's a characteristic that accurately reflects the image of a holy God. God does not have any skeletons in His closet. He doesn't have a single blemish on His character. He has never had a vulgar thought, made a coarse joke, or engaged in a lewd action. That's because those things would debase Him and others. God does only what builds others up and is worthy of praise.

He wants your life to be the same way—to be pure and worthy of praise—to be dazzling white in a world of pink and red. Take your dirty laundry to Him. He'll help you sort through it all, leaving you clean and whole inside and out.

Purpose

It is God who works in you to will and
to act according to his good purpose.

PHILIPPIANS 2:13

We know that God causes all things to work together for good
to those who love God, to those who are called
according to His purpose.

ROMANS 8:28 NASB

The one who plants and the one who waters have a common
purpose, and each will receive wages according to the labor of each.
For we are God's servants, working together; you are God's field,
God's building.

1 CORINTHIANS 3:8-9 NRSV

Whatever you do, work at it with all your heart,
as working for the LORD, not for men.

COLOSSIANS 3:23

We are God's [own] handiwork (His workmanship), recreated in
Christ Jesus, . . . that we may do those good works which God
predestined (planned beforehand) for us [taking paths which He
prepared ahead of time], that we should walk in them [living the
good life which He prearranged and made ready for us to live].

EPHESIANS 2:10 AMP

Heavenly Father,

Why am I here? What is my purpose in life? I know I'm not the first person to ask these questions; nevertheless, I am serious about wanting to know the answers. There has to be more to life than just the daily grind. At times, I feel like King Solomon when he grew cynical and said that all was vanity. Day in and day out, I often feel as if I'm running on a treadmill with no end in sight.

Inside I sense a stirring, a knowing that You are trying to get some things across to me. I want You to know that I am open to anything You want to show me. I love You and want to serve You. Take my life and do something with it.

Amen.

PURPOSE BY DESIGN

A hammer is designed to drive nails. A blender is designed to liquefy food. If you want to make a fruit smoothie, you could use a hammer to combine a banana, ice, juice, and a handful of blueberries—but it's not recommended. You'd be more likely to end up with a mushy mess than a refreshing beverage. Likewise, pounding in a picture hanger with the base of your blender isn't wise either. It's best to use a tool solely for the specific job it was designed to accomplish.

You are a complexly created, divinely designed, lavishly loved, wonderful woman. First and foremost, you were made to enjoy a relationship with God. You were also made to love and be loved, to worship, and to work. Though every child of God has these purposes in common, how each person lives them out will vary.

Although you are a woman of purpose and not a simple tool, keeping your one-of-a-kind design in mind will help you find where you fit best in this life. Your personality, temperament, talents, physical, mental, and emotional makeup are all part of your unique "shape." Understanding your God-given shape will help you choose how to spend your time and energy in ways that best support God's overall purposes for your life.

Every task, every job, every relationship, even every word that comes out of your mouth can help fulfill God's grand purpose for your life. Simply honor God, and how He created you, with the choices you make. He can use your unique design to make a wonderful difference in the world.

Precious Child,

Oh, yes! I do have a plan and purpose for your life, and it is greater than anything you can imagine! In fact, I encourage you to dream big. I often work through your desires to reveal My will, so be sure to write down the images that stir your soul, the ideas that grab your heart and fill it with hope and enthusiasm. I can't promise that My plan looks exactly like what you have in mind, but the seeds are there.

Each journey begins with a step, so today, take one step toward the future you dream of. Day by day, I will lead you. After a while, you will look back and see how the plan is taking shape. If you get off the path, I will nudge you to get back on. You are here on purpose—right here, right now.

Your loving Father

Quietness and Solitude

Be silent before the Sovereign LORD,
for the day of the LORD is near.
ZEPHANIAH 1:7

Very early in the morning, while it was still dark,
Jesus got up, left the house and went off to a solitary place,
where he prayed.
MARK 1:35

God says, "Be quiet and know that I am God."
PSALM 46:10 NCV

I wait quietly before God,
for my salvation comes from him.
PSALM 62:1 NLT

The effect of righteousness will be peace,
and the result of righteousness, quietness and trust forever.
My people will abide in a peaceful habitation,
in secure dwellings, and in quiet resting places.
ISAIAH 32:17-18 NRSV

STITCHED TOGETHER WITH SERENITY

A woman's life often resembles a patchwork quilt with mismatched scraps of commitments, relationships, hopes, fears, and the ever-present unexpected interruptions hastily sewn together with a large running stitch. Some seasons may be busier— and a bit more like a crazy quilt—than others. But even during the least-complicated and most under-control years of life, your periods of activity (i.e., chaos) will probably occur more frequently than natural periods of quiet and solitude.

Yet quiet and solitude are the border that helps keep the quilt of your life from coming apart at the seams. It is what frames your days with reflection, personal growth, and a sense of peace, enabling you to look toward the future with confidence, instead of with trepidation and exhaustion.

When your life is full, don't wait for quiet moments to find you. Openly invite them into your day. Get up fifteen minutes earlier in the morning, when your home and the world seem to be most tranquil, and just talk to God about the day ahead. Go for a brief walk during lunchtime, where you can be alone with your thoughts even if you happen to be surrounded by a crowd. Instead of turning on the TV in the evening, journal, read a chapter in a book, or relax in a candlelit bubble bath. Turn down the volume and slow the pace of your life in whatever little ways you can. Take every opportunity you can to stop and listen. God's voice and your own deepest thoughts are often spoken only in a whisper.

Redemption

With the LORD there is mercy,
And with Him is abundant redemption.
PSALM 130:7 NKJV

In Him we have redemption through His blood,
the forgiveness of sins, according to the riches of His grace.
EPHESIANS 1:7 NKJV

You know that it was not with perishable things such as silver
or gold that you were redeemed from the empty way of life
handed down to you from your forefathers, but with the
precious blood of Christ.
1 PETER 1:18-19

When someone becomes a Christian, he becomes a brand
new person inside. He is not the same any more. A new life
has begun! All these new things are from God who brought us
back to himself through what Christ Jesus did.
2 CORINTHIANS 5:17-18 TLB

He has delivered us from the power of darkness and conveyed
us into the kingdom of the Son of His love, in whom we have
redemption through His blood, the forgiveness of sins.
COLOSSIANS 1:13-14 NKJV

RANSOMED BY LOVE

Paint a joyful picture in your mind, one where you're holding someone you love close to your heart. Now picture how you would feel if that person were ripped away from your arms and a ransom demanded for his or her life. What would you do to come up with the money? Chances are you'd do anything and everything you could. You'd sell all you owned to assure your loved one's safe return. Your love for this person would compel you to do nothing less.

God's love compelled Him to do exactly the same thing for you. You are His precious child, and He loves you more deeply than any human parent ever could. Choosing to live life on your own ripped you out of your Father's arms. But there is no way you could afford to pay the high price required to return to His side.

As precious as you are, the price of your freedom is beyond anything mere money can buy. That's why you need a redeemer. In the Old Testament, a redeemer was someone who ransomed the life of a slave by paying a price the slave could not afford on his or her own. Jesus, God's only Son, is your Redeemer. He paid the price for your life not from His own pocket, but with His own blood. He gave His life for yours. That's what being ransomed by love is all about.

Why not take a moment to thank your Redeemer for all He's done for you because of love?

Rejection

Even if my father and mother abandon me,
the LORD will hold me close.

PSALM 27:10 NLT

The LORD will not reject his people;
he will never forsake his inheritance.

PSALM 94:14

The Lord says,
"I have chosen you and have not rejected you."

ISAIAH 41:9

Jesus said, "Those the Father has given me will come to me,
and I will never reject them."

JOHN 6:37 NLT

Jesus said, "The one who rejects you, rejects me.
And rejecting me is the same as rejecting God,
who sent me."

LUKE 10:16 MSG

Heavenly Father,

There it is again, the sting of rejection. Of all the emotions one can feel, I think rejection hurts the most. Sometimes I've felt rejected by people who intended to hurt me, but other times I've felt rejected even though no one was overtly trying to do so.

Whether it's through words or actions, or even just my overly sensitive emotions reading more into a situation than is really there, I ache. I feel alone and unworthy of those around me. If I'm honest with myself, at times I even feel that way about You.

Your Word says that You will never reject, and that is a great comfort. Sometimes, though, in my heart I'm just not sure. What if I fail You or disappoint You? Would You reject me then?

Amen.

NEVER AN OUTSIDER

The classroom door opens onto the playground, children spilling out from behind it in every direction, anxious for recess. But in a shadowed corner near the open door, one child remains silent and still. Lin Sue stands alone watching her classmates pair up with their friends, leaving her feeling like an old, unwanted toy—discarded, abandoned, and forgotten.

Lin Sue knew it wouldn't be easy fitting in at a new school. But she'd hoped that after a week or so she'd make a few friends. She'd hoped she'd fit in. Instead, when she is dropped off each morning, a group of boys mock her parents by trying to imitate the sounds of their foreign tongue. The lunches of rice and fish her mother carefully packs for her each day prompt classmates to roll their eyes and hold their noses. And the girl who sits next to her even makes fun of her name.

But every evening, Lin Sue's father draws her close. "Remember, Lin Sue," he says with great tenderness, "those children are rejecting someone they don't even know. No matter what happens, I will never turn away from you because I know who you are—someone worthy of great love and destined for great things."

You, too, have a Father who longs to draw you close—Someone who will never reject you, who knows exactly who you are, and who He created you to be—Someone who sees the best in you even though He knows the worst—Someone who has deemed you worthy of great love. Anytime you feel the sting of human rejection, draw close to your heavenly Father. He'll never turn away.

Precious Child,

Know for certain that I will never, ever reject you. Don't confuse the shortcomings of humans with Me and My nature. I planned for your birth before the foundation of the earth. I knit you together in your mother's womb, taking great pains to get every detail just right. I am the Master Craftsman, and I make no mistakes. You are uniquely formed for a specific purpose. No one can fulfill My plan for your life quite the way you can.

If anyone understands the pain of rejection, it is Jesus. He has felt every injury you've ever sustained, and He bore the pain of it for you. Receive His healing touch and allow it to mend your broken heart.

Never forget how precious you are to Me. You are My prized possession. I will never reject you.

Your loving Father

Relationships

Be humble and gentle. Be patient with each other, making
allowance for each other's faults because of your love.
EPHESIANS 4:2 TLB

Jesus said, "Let me give you a new command: Love one
another. In the same way I loved you, you love one another."
JOHN 13:34 MSG

Speak encouraging words to one another.
Build up hope so you'll all be together in this, no one left out,
no one left behind.
1 THESSALONIANS 5:11 MSG

Jesus said, "Here is a simple, rule-of-thumb guide for
behavior: Ask yourself what you want people to do for you,
then grab the initiative and do it for them."
MATTHEW 7:12 MSG

Laugh with your happy friends when they're happy;
share tears when they're down. Get along with each other;
don't be stuck-up. Make friends with nobodies;
don't be the great somebody.
ROMANS 12:15-16 MSG

GETTING UP CLOSE AND PERSONAL

Feeling lost in a sea of adults, the little dark-haired girl keeps her eyes on her feet as her mother continues to inch her closer toward the Teacher. "Can't you see the Teacher has more important things to do than bless your child?" one of Jesus' disciples retorts as the young woman and her daughter draw near.

Jesus stops in midconversation, reprimands the disciple with a glance, then kneels down on the rocky ground. Playfully, he tugs at one of the girl's ebony curls and whispers a few words in her ear. The young girl looks up shyly with a smile and then timidly climbs into His lap. As Jesus lays His hand ever so gently on the top of her head, He closes His eyes in prayer, asking His Father's blessing on one so small yet so precious.

Jesus spent time ministering to all kinds of people: church leaders, tax collectors, prostitutes, outcasts, people of all ages and from every walk of life. Though He spent the most time and built His strongest relationships with the disciples, He never ignored the others who were around Him. He recognized the significance of every individual and the potential of even a brief moment's interaction with another human being.

Relationships are built moment by moment. Whether you are conversing with a stranger at a bus stop or chatting with your dearest friend over a cup of coffee, relate to others as Jesus did. Be attentive. Be authentic. Be wise and loving and tender. Use every moment with others in a way that would make God smile.

Renewal

There must be a spiritual renewal of your thoughts and attitudes. You must display a new nature because you are a new person, created in God's likeness.

EPHESIANS 4:23-24 NLT

Create in me a pure heart, O God,
and renew a steadfast spirit within me.

PSALM 51:10

Those who wait for the Lord shall renew their strength,
they shall mount up with wings like eagles,
they shall run and not be weary,
they shall walk and not faint.

ISAIAH 40:31 NRSV

[The Lord] satisfies your desires with good things
so that your youth is renewed like the eagle's.

PSALM 103:5

We do not lose heart. Though our outer nature is wasting
away, our inner nature is being renewed every day.

2 CORINTHIANS 4:16 RSV

A BRAND-NEW CHAPTER

You've been on the waiting list for ages. Finally your name makes it to the top. You immediately head to your local library to pick up your much-anticipated summer read. You've heard it's amazing—a real page-turner. But then, life happens. The dog gets sick. The dishwasher breaks down. You get an extra assignment at work. The evenings you pictured in your mind—with you curled up in your favorite chair reading—are exchanged for a marathon of odds and ends that never seem to end. Before you know it, the book is due. With great courage and optimism you refuse defeat. You renew the book for another two weeks. You get a fresh start, a second chance, the new opportunity to do what your heart longs to do.

On occasion, life can be a great book you aren't taking the time to read. You may be distracted by details, weighed down by worries, overcommitted, overworked, or simply overwhelmed. God offers renewal. He provides you with a fresh new day each morning—a "second chance"—even if you've blown it many more times than twice.

If you're headed the wrong direction, stop. Take a fresh look at God. Allow Him to help you see yourself and your circumstances in a new, true light. Cast off yesterday and begin again. Leave your regrets, mistakes, and grudges by the wayside. It's time to turn a new page. There's a great and glorious story about a wonderful woman just waiting to be told.

Repentance

Don't you realize how patient he is being with you? . . . Can't you see that he has been waiting all this time without punishing you, to give you time to turn from your sin? His kindness is meant to lead you to repentance.

ROMANS 2:4 TLB

Repent! Turn away from all your offenses; then sin will not be your downfall. Rid yourselves of all the offenses you have committed, and get a new heart and a new spirit.

EZEKIEL 18:30-31

Jesus said, "There is forgiveness of sins for all who turn to me."

LUKE 24:47 NLT

This is what the LORD says:
"If you repent, I will restore you
that you may serve me."

JEREMIAH 15:19

. . . I am happy, not because you were made sorry, but because your sorrow led you to repentance. For you became sorrowful as God intended. . . . Godly sorrow brings repentance that leads to salvation and leaves no regret, but worldly sorrow brings death.

2 CORINTHIANS 7:9-10

Heavenly Father,

Once again I've blown it, and look where it has gotten me. Sometimes I wonder if I'll ever get it right. I start out okay and intend to follow You wholeheartedly. But then someone lets me down, and I get my feelings hurt; or the checkout lady is going too slow, and I get impatient.

Then there are the times when I intentionally go the wrong direction, not even caring about the consequences. I flippantly say to myself, *I'll repent later.* It's really hard to admit that one, but I've done it.

I'm ready to repent now, Lord. Please forgive me for my willfulness and help me to make better choices. I do love You and am so thankful for Your mercy and forgiveness. Help me make a fresh start.

Amen.

THE ROAD TO REPENTANCE

Imagine taking a road trip from Dallas, Texas, to Los Angeles, California. You hop in the car, head out to the highway, and then say to yourself, *You know, the road headed east looks much more inviting than the one going west.* So you take a right instead of a left. After driving a while, you don't seem to be getting any closer to the California coast, so you pull into a gas station to ask for directions.

You tell the attendant you want to go to Los Angeles. He points west. But you explain that you really would rather go east because it seems like a more pleasant drive. The attendant looks you straight in the eye and says, "Lady, how serious are you about getting to LA?"

The same kind of question could be asked when you head the opposite direction from where God has asked you to go: "How serious are you about getting close to God?" Everyone makes mistakes and poor choices on occasion. But if you're serious about following God, once you recognize you're headed the wrong direction you need to stop, turn around, and head the right direction. That's what repentance is. It's more than being sorry you've gone the wrong way because you've hurt both God and yourself. It's agreeing with God that you need to change direction—and then doing it.

Whether you consider your "detour" big or small is irrelevant. Even a road that leads slightly east will never take you west unless it turns back around. Ask God today if there's any area of your life that needs a change of direction. Then, don't make excuses. Turn around.

Precious Child,

Of course I'll forgive You. Although there are often natural consequences to sin, I will never turn you away when you repent. I know you are human and subject to human emotions and tendencies. You have a free will. When you choose to do right things, My heart is touched and blessed that you want to please Me.

However, I know you will sometimes choose to do wrong and go your own way. But like the father of the prodigal son, I will never give up on you or turn you away. When you come back to Me, My forgiveness will always be present to cleanse you of all sin and guilt.

I'm glad you've turned to go in My direction. Let's walk together now, hand in hand, heart-to-heart.

Your loving Father

Restoration

Since we were restored to friendship with God by the death of
his Son while we were still his enemies, we will certainly be
delivered from eternal punishment by his life.

ROMANS 5:10 NLT

The Lord replied,
"If you return to me, I will restore you so you can
continue to serve me."

JEREMIAH 15:19 NLT

[The Lord] restores my soul.
He leads me in paths of righteousness
for his name's sake.

PSALM 23:3 RSV

In his kindness God called you to his eternal glory
by means of Jesus Christ. After you have suffered a little while,
he will restore, support, and strengthen you, and he will place
you on a firm foundation.

1 PETER 5:10 NLT

Out of sheer generosity [God] put us in right standing with
himself. A pure gift. He got us out of the mess we're in and
restored us to where he always wanted us to be.

ROMANS 3:24 MSG

UNTOLD RICHES

You were crafted by the hands of a Master. You are like a rare gem carefully set and displayed on a fine gold chain: God meticulously joined every link of your physical, mental, and emotional being together before you were born. In you, God chose to create an individual of incomparable beauty and worth.

This is your true, God-given identity—you are a living, breathing, maturing jewel, a treasure that's guarded and cherished by your Creator and King. However, not every woman sees herself for who she is. Some women view themselves more as costume jewelry than as priceless riches. How you view yourself will affect how you treat yourself and how you allow others to treat you. If you feel like worthless fool's gold, you're liable to end up cast off in a careless heap, your gold chain knotted and your precious stone chipped and marred. But that doesn't change who you really are.

God longs to restore you to your natural luster. This process begins when you agree with what God has to say in His Word about your true identity. Once you have a clear picture of how valuable you are to God and how much He has sacrificed because of His love for you, you can be fully open with Him about how far you've fallen away from His original design.

Through forgiveness and grace, you and God can begin to work hand in hand. Together, you can gently get the kinks out of your chain. You can patiently polish the priceless jewel of your heart until it's returned to its original flawless brilliance. Only then will your true beauty be evident as God's reflection becomes visible in every facet of your design.

Resurrection

Jesus said, "I . . . am the resurrection and the life. Those who believe in me will have life even if they die. And everyone who lives and believes in me will never die."

JOHN 11:25-26 NCV

We were buried with Him through baptism into death, that just as Christ was raised from the dead by the glory of the Father, even so we also should walk in newness of life. For if we have been united together in the likeness of His death, certainly we also shall be in the likeness of His resurrection.

ROMANS 6:4-5 NKJV

Praise be to the God and Father of our LORD Jesus Christ! In his great mercy he has given us new birth into a living hope through the resurrection of Jesus Christ from the dead, and into an inheritance that can never perish, spoil or fade—kept in heaven for you.

1 PETER 1:3-4

If the Spirit of Him who raised Jesus from the dead dwells in you, He who raised Christ from the dead will also give life to your mortal bodies through His Spirit who dwells in you.

ROMANS 8:11 NKJV

RISEN

Tabitha opens her eyes from what feels like a heavy sleep. A man she's never met takes her gently by the hand to help her rise from the wooden table she's reclining on. *An odd place to fall asleep*, she thinks. Then she notices what she's wearing. In place of her usual garment, similar to the countless robes she has sewn to clothe the poor, Tabitha finds herself wrapped in a shroud. Tabitha begins to question the young man, but with a mischievous smile, he holds a finger to his lips, requesting silence.

Tabitha loosens her burial clothes and steps down from the table. As she passes through the doorway of the upstairs room, Tabitha hears muffled sobs coming from below. Descending the stairs, she catches sight of the crowd—family and friends over-flowing out of the house and into the courtyard. Immediately, the sobs are transformed into shouts of joy. An astonished chorus of "She's alive!" and "Praise God!" fills the room, spilling laughter and praise out into the streets.

Jesus isn't the only One to rise from the dead. Through the power of prayer, the apostle Peter brought Tabitha back to life (Acts 9:36-42). Elisha resurrected a widow's son (2 Kings 54:32-37). Jesus revived the life of a little girl (Luke 8:54-55), a young man, and His dear friend Lazarus (John 11:43-44). Though all of these people were given a miraculous second chance at life, they would each face a second death here on earth.

Jesus is the only One who has ever risen from the dead—and never died again. Through the power of His resurrection you will rise after death to your new life in heaven—a life without end.

Righteousness

For our sake he made him to be sin who knew no sin, so that in
him we might become the righteousness of God.

2 CORINTHIANS 5:21 RSV

[The Lord] blesses the home of the righteous.

PROVERBS 3:33

The mouth of the righteous is a fountain of life.

PROVERBS 10:11 NRSV

The tongue of the righteous is choice silver. . . .
The lips of the righteous nourish many. . . .
The mouth of the righteous brings forth wisdom. . . .
The lips of the righteous know what is fitting.

PROVERBS 10:20-21,31-32

The kingdom of God is not a matter of eating and drinking,
but of righteousness, peace and joy in the Holy Spirit, because
anyone who serves Christ in this way is pleasing to God.

ROMANS 14:17-18

Heavenly Father,

"Righteousness" sounds like such a lofty term—and impossible to achieve. With all of my shortcomings, how can I ever attain right standing with You? When I think of righteous people, I think of people such as Mother Teresa, who sacrificed all the trappings of a normal life to serve You, and also Billy Graham, who has conducted massive crusades and won an enormous number of people to You. It's easy to imagine that people like them are righteous because of all the good things they have done.

But what about someone like me? How could I possibly measure up to these spiritual giants? Will I ever be righteous enough to please You and secure my place in heaven?

Amen.

WHAT WOULD JESUS DO?

The wooden bench feels harder to Lorraine at the end of a long day. She glances down the street for what feels like the hundredth time—still no bus. But something else catches her eye. He's an older man with a white cane, wearing a trench coat and carrying a small bag of groceries with his free hand. He's surrounded by a group of young boys. Stifling laughter, they walk next to him, imitating his rhythmic gait with exaggerated movements, then shifting in front of him to make mocking faces—faces that his eyes can no longer see.

The man knows something or someone is near and calls out, but the boys only answer with more silent taunting. Lorraine wants to stay on the bench with the others—a mere observer, safe, uninvolved. But compassion pulls her to her feet. "Excuse me," she calls out to the boys, still unsure of what to say. "What if this gentleman were your father or brother or best friend?"

The boys direct a rude comment her way. Then they take off down the street at a full run. As the man continues toward her, she sees a single tear on his cheek. "Thank you," he says in almost a whisper. "Thank you so much."

Doing what pleases God is the natural result of being made the righteousness of God in Christ. It can also motivate you to refrain from doing something you know is wrong. When in doubt, just follow Jesus' example. The closer you follow Him, the more your heart begins to resemble His—and His righteousness can be given full rein.

Precious Child,

You're right. Righteousness is an awesome thing, but did you know that no person is capable of being truly righteous? In fact, in My Word I say that humanity's righteousness is like filthy rags to Me.

But before you get discouraged, let Me explain. I knew that no one could possibly achieve a righteous status due to the sin nature inherent in humans. This is one of the main reasons that I sent My Son. Jesus paid the penalty for your sin so that you could be made righteous. He actually became your sin, and when you received Him, you became His righteousness—a divine exchange. You are righteous right now!

No number of good deeds could have earned your righteousness, but because you have been made righteous, good deeds naturally flow from your born-again spirit. And as for heaven, let's just say I'm counting the days till you can join me.

Your loving Father

Sacrifice

I will not sacrifice to the LORD my God burnt offerings
that cost me nothing.

2 SAMUEL 24:24

May he remember all your offerings
and accept all your sacrifices.

PSALM 20:3 NCV

We know love by this, that he laid down his life for us—and we
ought to lay down our lives for one another. How does God's
love abide in anyone who has the world's goods and sees a
brother or sister in need and yet refuses help?

1 JOHN 3:16-17 NRSV

Put your trust in the Lord, and offer him pleasing sacrifices.

PSALM 4:5 TLB

Brothers and sisters, since God has shown us great mercy,
I beg you to offer your lives as a living sacrifice to him.

ROMANS 12:1 NCV

God said, "He who offers a sacrifice
of thanksgiving honors Me."

PSALM 50:23 NASB

YOU'RE DEEPLY LOVED

Chances are, you know what it feels like to sacrifice something that means a lot to you. Maybe you've sacrificed your time to volunteer in your community. Perhaps you've sacrificed some of your freedom to care for an ailing parent. Sacrificing something that's precious to you for the benefit of someone else isn't easy— even if you love that person deeply. But you persevere because you believe it's the right and loving thing to do.

Where your future is concerned, Jesus believed that no sacrifice was too great to make sure you would spend eternity with Him in heaven. That's why Jesus gave up His life for you on the cross. He invited suffering and separation from His heavenly Father into His life for the good of your life.

For just a moment, put yourself in Jesus' sandals. It's true that Jesus is God, but while here on earth, He was also fully human. What would it take for you to give up your life for someone else? How deep would your love have to be? What if the one you were sacrificing your life for not only wasn't grateful, but couldn't care less about you?

You won't be able to fully understand the true cost of Jesus' sacrifice until you meet Him face-to-face. Until then, don't let a day go by without reminding yourself of the depth of Jesus' love for you. Allow His sacrifice to fill your heart with thanks and inspire you toward loving God and others more deeply—even when it costs you.

Seeking God

"You will call upon Me and go and pray to Me,
and I will listen to you. And you will seek Me and find Me,
when you search for Me with all your heart. I will be found
by you," says the LORD.
JEREMIAH 29:12-14 NKJV

All who seek the Lord shall find him and
shall praise his name.
PSALM 22:26 TLB

The humble shall see their God at work for them. No wonder
they will be so glad! All who seek for God shall live in joy.
PSALM 69:32 TLB

Seek the Lord while you can find him.
Call upon him now while he is near.
ISAIAH 55:6 TLB

Jesus said, "Ask, and it will be given you; seek,
and you will find; knock, and it will be opened to you.
For every one who asks receives, and he who seeks finds, and
to him who knocks it will be opened."
MATTHEW 7:7-8 RSV

LOOKING FOR LOVE IN ALL THE RIGHT PLACES

When you were a little girl, playing hide-and-seek may have been an entertaining way to spend an afternoon with siblings or friends. As an adult, you probably don't have the time or interest to play a childish game such as that—particularly with the God of the universe. The good news is, you don't have to. Just because God asks you to seek Him doesn't mean He's hiding from you. As a matter of fact, God promises in Scripture that if you do look for Him, you'll find Him—no game playing. You seek and you find—guaranteed.

God is not lost and in need of being found. People are the ones who get lost. They lose their way to God by seeking things other than Him to make their lives work. They seek satisfaction and significance through their work, families, possessions, or pleasures. But only by seeking God is true love—and true life—ever found.

Seeking an invisible God may seem like a difficult task in a world where your five senses rule. But you don't have to open cabinets, look under beds, or listen for bumps in the night to discern where He is. God is right here, right now. When you call out to Him, He hears you. When you read the Bible, you more clearly see who God is and how His hand is active in this world. When you act in ways that reflect God's image within you, you become more aware of His presence in every aspect of your life. Only by seeking God will you find what your heart truly longs for.

Sincerity

Now that you have purified your souls by your obedience to the
truth so that you have genuine mutual love, love one another deeply
from the heart. . . . Rid yourselves, therefore, of all malice, and all
guile, insincerity, envy, and all slander.

1 PETER 1:22; 2:1 NRSV

Let us come near to God with a sincere heart and a sure faith,
because we have been made free from a guilty conscience, and our
bodies have been washed with pure water.

HEBREWS 10:22 NCV

In everything we have done in the world, and especially with you, we
have had an honest and sincere heart from God. We did this by
God's grace, not by the kind of wisdom the world has.

2 CORINTHIANS 1:12 NCV

May God's grace and blessing be upon all who sincerely
love our Lord Jesus Christ.

EPHESIANS 6:24 TLB

Lord, who may go and find refuge and shelter
in your tabernacle up on your holy hill?
Anyone who leads a blameless life and is truly sincere.

PSALM 15:1-2 TLB

Heavenly Father,

My heart's cry is to be a genuinely sincere person, one who loves You from a pure heart. So often, though, my motivation for doing things is far from that. I hate to admit it, but sometimes I serve You solely out of obligation. Other times it's the approval of people that I seek. Sometimes I'm just trying to feel good about myself. Oh, how that must grieve You.

In Your Word, You compare hypocritical people to whitewashed tombs that appear beautiful on the outside but are full of dead men's bones. Is that what I look like when my motivation has been corrupted?

Father, I do love You—sincerely and from the bottom of my heart. Help me to keep my motives pure. Prod me to take stock when I slip back into my prideful ways.

Amen.

A GIFT FROM THE HEART

Love, gratitude, worship—Mary's feelings toward Jesus go so much deeper than she can adequately express. Jesus' words make her feel alive and whole. He miraculously raised her brother from the dead (John 11:43-44). He calls her "friend" and she now calls Him "Lord." How can she honor Him? How can she let Him know what's in her heart?

All Mary can think of is to grab her most valuable possession— a jar of expensive perfume worth nearly a year's wages. The family has carefully set it aside as a safeguard, something to be sold in time of need. But Mary's need to honor Jesus is greater than her desire for financial security. The conversation of the disciples and other dinner guests comes to a sudden halt as Mary shatters the lid of the alabaster jar (Luke 7:36-40). As the fragrance of her offering fills the room, Mary lovingly pours the perfume over Jesus' head, anointing Him as one worthy of great honor—or as a body being prepared for burial.

The guests rebuke Mary's impulsive act, criticizing her extravagance. The perfume could have been sold and the profits donated to the poor! But Jesus defends Mary's action as a sincere act of love.

Following your heart can look foolish to those who don't share your devotion. But God sees your sincerity. He knows your desire to honor Him. He understands when love compels you to do something "just because." While you need to think things through and act wisely, you can lock yourself into inaction with the paralysis of analysis. When pure motives from a sincere heart lead you toward doing something that benefits another, don't overanalyze. Love extravagantly.

Precious Child,

No one wants to be loved out of a sense of duty. Besides, can that really be considered love?

Take the Pharisees in the Bible. They prided themselves in keeping the Law. They memorized My Word but then used it as a club to proclaim their superiority and put others down. They performed good deeds, but they did so with great fanfare so they could receive the applause of men. And they prayed—loudly and often—but they made such a spectacle of it that it was merely for show. They did all these good things, but their hearts were far from Me.

It was—and still is—the motivation behind actions that counts. The fact that you even want to serve Me out of a sincere and pure heart touches Me deeply. You are precious to Me, and I am pleased with you.

Your loving Father

Spiritual Growth

We are joined together in his body by his strong sinews,
and we grow only as we get our nourishment and
strength from God.

COLOSSIANS 2:19 NLT

As newborn babes, desire the pure milk of the word,
that you may grow thereby.

1 PETER 2:2 NKJV

Jesus said, "What is the seed that fell on the good ground?
That seed is like the person who hears the teaching and
understands it. That person grows and produces fruit."

MATTHEW 13:23 NCV

We must become like a mature person, growing until we
become like Christ and have his perfection. . . .
Speaking the truth with love, we will grow up in every way
into Christ, who is the head.

EPHESIANS 4:13,15 NCV

When you proclaim [God's] truth in everyday speech, you're
letting others in on the truth so that they can grow and be
strong and experience his presence with you.

1 CORINTHIANS 14:3 MSG

HOW DOES YOUR GARDEN GROW?

A thin blanket of snow covers the ground. The tree branches are bare and lifeless. Not a hint of blue cracks through the slate-hued sky. Everything is the color of an antique photo, a still life rendered in shades of gray. And as for the garden planted in your front yard, it looks more like a cemetery, frozen in time—a monument that seems to speak only of the past and not the future.

Then, the miracle occurs. One morning, a brilliant amethyst-colored bulb erupts from its slumber beneath the surface of the half-frozen soil. The first bud of spring heralds the promise of so many more, a reminder that growth happens as much below the surface as it does aboveground—both in the garden and in your soul.

Your spiritual life has seasons just like those of the physical world. Some days you may be joyfully aware of the brand-new blossoms pushing up through the earth. Other days you may find yourself in the throes of winter, wondering if the hard ground of your soul will ever change, if you will ever be who God has created you to be. But growth happens only one day at a time. A beautiful blossom cannot be rushed into maturity.

If you find yourself in a "waiting" season, keep tending your spiritual soil. Weed through your thoughts and activities, getting rid of what might choke the tender life out of new buds of faith. Keep your spiritual ground well watered with prayer. Cultivate future growth by risking new relationships, particularly those that support your own relationship with God. Then, watch diligently for signs of spring. It's on its way.

Strength

The Lord said to me, "My grace is sufficient for you, for my power is made perfect in weakness." Therefore I will boast all the more gladly about my weaknesses, so that Christ's power may rest on me. That is why, for Christ's sake, I delight in weaknesses. . . . For when I am weak, then I am strong.

2 CORINTHIANS 12:9-10

I pray that from his glorious, unlimited resources he will give you mighty inner strength through his Holy Spirit.

EPHESIANS 3:16 NLT

May our Lord Jesus Christ and God our Father, who loved us and in his special favor gave us everlasting comfort and good hope, comfort your hearts and give you strength in every good thing you do and say.

2 THESSALONIANS 2:16-17 NLT

Those who hope in the LORD
will renew their strength.
They will soar on wings like eagles;
they will run and not grow weary,
they will walk and not be faint.

ISAIAH 40:31

STRENGTH FOR EVERY BATTLE

A single drop of rain grazes Deborah's cheek. As a drizzle becomes a downpour, Deborah's lips break into a smile, then overflow with words of praise. From her vantage point on the hill, Deborah watches the Kishon River flood its banks as the seasonably dry ground is transformed into a muddy trap, paralyzing the Canaanite chariots. The enemy's army flees in defeat, assisted by the oncoming Israelite swords but conquered by the hand of God himself—the same almighty hand that has directed Deborah down a controversial path as a prophetess, a judge, and now a military leader (Judg. 4:4-16).

At times, Deborah has doubted her own strength to take on such an unconventional role for an Israelite woman, but she has never doubted God's power to accomplish His plan. He is her strength through every battle, both without and within.

True strength is not measured by the size of your muscles but by the conviction of your heart. It takes courage to follow God down unexpected paths, to obey Him when it would be easier to just follow the crowd, to persevere when you can't see the finish line. But when your heart is set on pursuing a relationship with God, you tap into a greater source of strength than your own. You join hands with the Creator of the universe. Surely nothing is too hard for Him.

Working together, God will help you attain victories you could never achieve on your own. When you face a battle of any kind, don't hesitate to reach out and lean fully on God. He will provide the strength you need to do whatever He asks you to do.

Thankfulness

In everything give thanks;
for this is the will of God in Christ Jesus for you.

1 THESSALONIANS 5:18 NKJV

By Him let us continually offer the sacrifice of praise to God, that
is, the fruit of our lips, giving thanks to His name.

HEBREWS 13:15 NKJV

The LORD is my strength and my shield;
my heart trusts in him, and I am helped.
My heart leaps for joy
and I will give thanks to him in song.

PSALM 28:7

I will give thee thanks in the great congregation:
I will praise thee among much people.

PSALM 35:18 KJV

It is good to give thanks to the LORD,
And to sing praises to Your name, O Most High;
To declare Your lovingkindness in the morning,
And Your faithfulness every night.

PSALM 92:1-2 NKJV

Heavenly Father,

When I consider all of the wonderful things You have done for me, my heart is filled with thanksgiving. Sure, there are things I could gripe about, but why would I want to dwell on them? Besides, You promise to perfect everything that concerns me and to work everything out for my good, so negative circumstances are subject to change.

Thank You for the freedoms I enjoy every day, the miraculous way my body performs, and the eternal treasures waiting for me in heaven. My friends and family are priceless as is the love and encouragement they provide. The gifts and talents You've woven into my being are beautiful, and I offer them back to You to glorify Your name. You've abundantly supplied my needs for food, clothing, and shelter—and on and on and on.

Thank You for all Your goodness to me, Father. I love You.

Amen.

THE GIFT OF GRATITUDE

Every day is not too often to write a thank-you note to God in prayer. Consider your family, your friends, your health, your home, your job, your church, the food in your refrigerator, the clothes in your closet, the car in your garage, the country you live in, the freedom you enjoy, the talents God's given you, the love He's lavished on you, the forgiveness He's extended to you, the grace He's showered on you—just for starters.

Then, recall His promises. God has assured you His joy, peace, presence, salvation, wisdom, blessing, strength, comfort, patience, faithfulness, protection, encouragement, guidance, courage, healing, everlasting life, Spirit, and answers to prayer. The list of reasons to say thanks is as endless as eternity itself.

Each moment is a gift straight from heaven. That means every moment holds the potential for praise. The more often you stop to thank God for all He's done for you, the more reasons you'll find you have to be thankful.

It's hard for negative feelings and a pessimistic perspective to take root in a heart that has been well cultivated with gratitude. There's just not enough room for despair, disappointment, and discontentment to grow. That means that while you're honoring God by thanking Him, you're also benefiting yourself by lifting your own spirits.

Gratitude is a gift to both God and yourself, and it's one that is easy to give. Why not take a moment right now to express your thanks to the One who has given you so much?

Precious Child,

It blesses Me that your heart is so filled with gratitude. Often people take their blessings for granted, and they don't see that I am behind everything good that happens to them. But that is not the case with you. You do notice and are quick to praise Me for every little thing. That blesses My heart, and I am moved to shower you with more.

A thankful heart is a happy heart, and it is one of the ways that you show forth My glory. When others see the smile on your face and the skip in your step, they realize there is something different about you. That difference, as you know, is Me. Help others to recognize My hand of blessing in their lives and introduce them to the joy of thankfulness.

Your loving Father

Thoughts

Those who live following their sinful selves think only about things that their sinful selves want. But those who live following the Spirit are thinking about the things the Spirit wants them to do. If people's thinking is controlled by the sinful self, there is death. But if their thinking is controlled by the Spirit, there is life and peace.

ROMANS 8:5-6 NCV

I am always thinking of the Lord; and because he is so near, I never need to stumble or to fall.

PSALM 16:8 TLB

Be careful what you think, because your thoughts run your life.

PROVERBS 4:23 NCV

Fix your thoughts on what is true and honorable and right. Think about things that are pure and lovely and admirable. Think about things that are excellent and worthy of praise.

PHILIPPIANS 4:8 NLT

As he thinks in his heart, so is he.

PROVERBS 23:7 NKJV

CHANGE YOUR MIND

When you're serious about losing weight, it's best to avoid certain situations, like trolling the glass shelves of your favorite bakery or loading up the freezer with gallons of ice cream. Knowing where your weaknesses lie and keeping temptations out of your reach can help you become more successful in maintaining a healthy lifestyle.

The same strategy works with your mind. The world offers an enticing buffet of mental junk food. Filling your thoughts with gruesome images, empty philosophies, unrelenting negativity, and moral ambiguity can weaken your relationship with God. Like empty calories, these things may seem enjoyable at first—harmless guilty pleasures. But a constant diet of R-rated entertainment, gossip-filled relationships, worry, and criticism will sabotage a healthy mind as sure as snacking on pork rinds will sabotage a healthy diet.

In the same way that eating wholesome food helps maintain a healthy body, viewing, reading, and listening to wholesome movies, TV, books, music, and conversations can help keep your thoughts directed toward healthier, more positive, God-honoring things.

So, fill your mind with good things. Dwell on the positive instead of the negative. If you can't picture God enjoying what you're watching, reading, or listening to, turn off the TV, get rid of the book, or change radio stations. If worry starts to build in your mind, change the direction of your thoughts by turning your worries into prayers. Maintain a steady diet of God's words by both reading and memorizing Scripture. The more positive things you put into your mind, the less appetite you'll find you have for anything less.

Time

See then that you walk circumspectly,
not as fools but as wise, redeeming the time.
EPHESIANS 5:15-16 NKJV

We've finally figured it out. Our lives get in step with God and
all others by letting him set the pace, not by proudly or
anxiously trying to run the parade.
ROMANS 3:28 MSG

To every thing there is a season,
and a time to every purpose under the heaven.
ECCLESIASTES 3:1 KJV

Don't procrastinate—
there's no time to lose.
PROVERBS 6:4 MSG

Jesus said, "Are you tired? Worn out? . . . Come to me.
Get away with me and you'll recover your life. I'll show you
how to take a real rest. Walk with me and work with me—watch
how I do it. Learn the unforced rhythms of grace. I won't lay
anything heavy or ill-fitting on you. Keep company with me
and you'll learn to live freely and lightly."
MATTHEW 11:28-30 MSG

KNOW YOUR LIMITS

God not only gives you a road map but a speed limit for living. Your life is like a modern freeway: God sets both minimum and maximum speeds that help keep everyone moving safely toward their destinations. But God's maximum and minimum speed limits differ from person to person. Your natural pace may be as speedy as that of a roadrunner or as slow as that of a sloth. It all depends on the way God designed you.

Some people work against God's design. Some try to cram five days' worth of work into one by living on caffeine, adrenaline, and too little sleep. Others barely move forward at all by sacrificing much of their day on the altar of procrastination, fear, selfishness, or downright laziness.

The key to using time well is to live at the speed God designed you to live by doing what He designed you to do. When you keep God's priorities in mind as you schedule your day, you'll find that work, rest, family, friendships, serving others, and even watching TV can all fit into a balanced, healthy life. There may be times when things get overly hectic or when you have a block of free time to sit back and do nothing, but these are the exception and not the rule for both roadrunners and sloths.

Both a roadrunner and a sloth have the same twenty-four hours each day. That's nonnegotiable. But no one, other than God, knows how many of those days will add up to a lifetime. Use each day wisely, keeping your pace and your purpose always in mind.

Trials

Whenever you face trials of any kind, consider it nothing but joy, because you know that the testing of your faith produces endurance; and let endurance have its full effect, so that you may be mature and complete, lacking in nothing.

JAMES 1:2-4 NRSV

Be truly glad! There is wonderful joy ahead, even though it is necessary for you to endure many trials for a while. These trials are only to test your faith, to show that it is strong and pure. It is being tested as fire tests and purifies gold. . . . So if your faith remains strong after being tried by fiery trials, it will bring you much praise and glory and honor on the day when Jesus Christ is revealed to the whole world.

1 PETER 1:6-7 NLT

No test or temptation that comes your way is beyond the course of what others have had to face. All you need to remember is that God will never let you down; he'll never let you be pushed past your limit; he'll always be there to help you come through it.

1 CORINTHIANS 10:13 MSG

We can rejoice . . . when we run into problems and trials, for we know that they are good for us—they help us learn to endure.

ROMANS 5:3 NLT

Heavenly Father,

I need Your help. I am so oppressed because of this trial I am going through. I feel as if I've been thrown into the fiery furnace and I forgot to wear my flame-retardant suit. You promised never to let me go through more than I can bear, but how much more can I take?

Forgive me, Father, for letting the circumstances get to me. This isn't the first difficult season I've encountered. There have been others, and I felt just as discouraged and overwhelmed as I do now. But You've never let me down. At the time I couldn't always see it, but as the days and weeks played out, I began to see how You faithfully guided me through each and every trial. Psalm 34:19 says, "Many are the afflictions of the righteous, / but the Lord rescues them from them all" (NRSV). I trust You to rescue me again.

Amen.

UNEXPECTED JOURNEY

There are two ways you can look at trials. You can regard them as roadblocks on the highway of life, or you can choose to view them as "taking the scenic route." While life's inevitable struggles don't feel as comfortable as those carefree days when everything goes as planned, they can take you places you could never go without them—places with a purpose that will bring you to a deeper, fuller life with God.

Just look at the life of Joseph in the Old Testament. He was the favorite son, so his jealous brothers threw him into a well, then sold him as a slave (Gen. 37:23-28). Thanks to his hard work and God's favor, Joseph ended up employed in the home of a high-ranking Egyptian official (Gen. 39:1). But when Joseph rightly rebuffed the advances of the official's wife, she accused him of raping her—and Joseph wound up in prison (vv. 7-20). After becoming known for accurately interpreting dreams, Joseph interpreted a dream for Pharaoh—a dream that saved Egypt from famine and put Joseph back into an influential position (Gen. 41:14-45). When Joseph's brothers, suffering from the famine, came to beg Pharaoh for help, they not only wound up with food but were reconciled with their long-lost brother (Gen. 42,45).

God used very difficult trials in Joseph's life to guide him along a scenic route. For Joseph, the journey must have seemed long and arduous at times. But after his family was reunited, Joseph certainly looked back and saw God's hand at work every step of the way.

Whether you can see God's hand at work or have to keep moving ahead by faith, remember there's hidden treasure in struggle. You never know the amazing places your scenic route may lead.

Precious Child,

I know exactly what you are going through and how you feel. When Jesus suffered on the cross, He took on all of your pains, physical and emotional. He is an understanding and compassionate High Priest.

All that said, I want to assure you that I am at work in this situation, even though you may not be able to see it. I am causing everything to work out for the ultimate best in your life. Your part is to keep your heart right—walk in love toward others and trust Me fully, keeping My promises before your eyes. The circumstances you are encountering are real, but the truth in My Word will change any earthly circumstance. Just as Shadrach, Meshach, and Abednego escaped the fiery furnace untouched, you will too. Not a hair on your head will be singed.

Your loving Father

Truth

The Lord's promise is sure. He speaks no careless word;
all he says is purest truth, like silver seven times refined.
PSALM 12:6 TLB

A wise person is hungry for truth,
while the fool feeds on trash.
PROVERBS 15:14 NLT

Truth stands the test of time.
PROVERBS 12:19 NLT

Our responsibility is never to oppose the truth,
but to stand for the truth at all times.
2 CORINTHIANS 13:8 NLT

Cross-examine me, O Lord, and see that this is so;
test my motives and affections too. For I have taken your
lovingkindness and your truth as my ideals.
PSALM 26:2-3 TLB

Jesus said, "You will know the truth,
and the truth will set you free."
JOHN 8:32 NLT

ONE HUNDRED PERCENT GENUINE

Nonfat cheese is an imposter. It doesn't slice like real cheese. It doesn't melt like real cheese. Most importantly, it doesn't taste like real cheese. Yes, you can get used to it after a while. You can put it on a sandwich and call it "grilled cheese," but it can't provide that buttery, gooey goodness you enjoyed as a kid. It simply doesn't have what it takes—fat.

Truth is the same way. You can water it down, tweak a few details, replace a few facts, and call it "truth," but that doesn't make it true. One taste, and you'll know something's missing, something's not quite right. You can acquire a taste for it over time, but just because you grow to like it doesn't change what it is— a lie. Truth doesn't come in low fat or nonfat. It's either wholly true or it's false.

God always tells the truth. He doesn't play word games or try to spin a story a certain way to make people like Him better. He doesn't have to. His truth is compelling enough to stand on its own. When He says He loves you, there are no ifs, ands, or buts. When He says you're forgiven, it's the truth, the whole truth, and nothing but the truth. When you're looking for a gauge to deter-mine whether something is true or not, compare it to God's Word. If it contradicts Scripture, there's something untrue about it. It may sound good. It may look good. But in the end, it will never satisfy your craving for the real thing.

Vision

This is GOD'S Word on the subject: " . . . I know what I'm doing. I have it all planned out—plans to take care of you, not abandon you, plans to give you the future you hope for."

JEREMIAH 29:10-11 MSG

Don't shuffle along, eyes to the ground, absorbed with the things right in front of you. Look up, and be alert to what is going on around Christ—that's where the action is. See things from his perspective.

COLOSSIANS 3:2 MSG

I keep the LORD always before me;
because he is at my right hand, I shall not be moved.
Therefore my heart is glad, and my soul rejoices.

PSALM 16:8-9 RSV

Many are the afflictions of the righteous,
but the Lord rescues them from them all.

PSALM 34:19 NRSV

Jesus said, "What is impossible from a human perspective
is possible with God."

LUKE 18:27 NLT

BEYOND CIRCUMSTANCE

The Christian's Secret of a Happy Life is a book title that's bound to pique your interest. After all, who wouldn't want to grab hold of the key to happiness? If you had the opportunity to change places with the author, to walk in her shoes and experience the joy she found in her life, you might be tempted to take it—until you took a look at the life this author lived.

Hannah Whitall Smith lived in the mid-1800s. She was married at the age of nineteen to a man who suffered from manic depression. Early in their marriage, he preached to crowds throughout Europe and the United States. But soon he abandoned his faith, and his fidelity, in very public ways. Hannah remained faithful to her husband and gave birth to seven children. Four died young. Of her three remaining children, one daughter abandoned her husband and children, fleeing to Italy to live with her lover. Another daughter married Bertrand Russell, a British philosopher and mathematician who spent much of his life vehemently opposing Christianity—and his mother-in-law and her beliefs.

Obviously, Hannah's secret to living a happy life was not dependent on her circumstances. Instead, she found her happiness in seeing beyond them. Hannah didn't view life through rose-colored glasses, but through God's eyes. She was a woman of vision, a woman who kept an eternal perspective on temporal troubles. When you see your circumstances and the people around you through a filter of God's love, grace, and eternal purpose, then you will find yourself on the road to a happy life.

Wisdom

To get wisdom is to love oneself.

PROVERBS 19:8 NRSV

King Solomon . . . wrote [these proverbs] to teach his people how
to live—how to act in every circumstance, for he wanted them to be
understanding, just and fair.

PROVERBS 1:1-3 TLB

Wisdom is the principal thing. . . .
Exalt her, and she will promote you;
She will bring you honor, when you embrace her.

PROVERBS 4:7-8 NKJV

Wisdom will make your life pleasant
and will bring you peace. . . .
Everyone who uses it will be happy.

PROVERBS 3:17-18 NCV

There's nothing better than being wise. . . .
Wisdom puts light in the eyes,
And gives gentleness to words and manners.

ECCLESIASTES 8:1 MSG

Heavenly Father,

I really need Your help right now. I am confronted with some important issues, and I've been wringing my hands trying to figure out the best thing to do. What I need is Your wisdom because it is the only way to ensure that Your will is accomplished and that there is a favorable outcome. My own human wisdom can't always be trusted, but Your ways are higher than mine and You see things that I don't. I am comforted when I realize that You know the future better than I even know the past.

So help me to hear Your voice, Father, and guide me as I search Your Word. It is a lamp to my feet and a light to my path. Let Your wisdom prevail.

Amen.

WISE WORDS

The king's court grows silent as two women enter the room clutching one newborn baby between them. Easily recognizable as prostitutes, each woman's accusation echoes the other. They have both given birth to sons three days apart. One son died in his sleep. One mother exchanged her dead child for the living child in the other sleeping mother's arms. "The child is mine!" one cries out as the other angrily replies, "She's lying! He's mine!"

The king's answer? "Cut the child in half and give one half to each woman." One woman responds coldly, "Fine!" The other falls to her knees, pleading, "Don't kill him! Give the baby to her!" (I Kings 3:16-27). A mother's compassion reveals the truth. A king's wisdom discerns how to rule justly.

That king was Solomon, the son of David, heralded as being the wisest man who ever lived. When God offered Solomon anything he wanted, instead of riches or power or even a long life, Solomon chose wisdom. Of course, being wise and choosing to act wisely don't always go hand in hand. As wise as Solomon was, he chose to ignore God's instructions about marriage. In the end, Solomon's large harem of foreign wives ended up turning the king's heart away from the God, who had given him so much.

God invites you to ask Him for wisdom as Solomon did. He can help you discern what is the best course of action for any situation you face. But the choice is up to you whether or not you put that wisdom into action. Intelligence, wealth, position, and even good health can all be squandered without wisdom. Put wisdom to work in your life today.

Precious Child,

I don't like to see you get so worked up about things, although I do understand there's a lot at stake regarding the situations you are dealing with. But when you allow anxiety to get a foothold, it makes it very difficult for you to hear My voice.

So find a quiet place and still your mind. Worshiping Me will help you to focus on spiritual things rather than all the natural circumstances, and it will open up your heart. Then begin to read your Bible, inviting the Holy Spirit to enlighten you and give you discernment. Jot down any thoughts that come to you as you read.

You can recognize My wisdom because it is always peaceable. It might not make sense to your natural mind, but deep down inside you will have a peace that passes your under-standing.

Your loving Father

Work

Easy come, easy go,
but steady diligence pays off.
PROVERBS 13:11 MSG

Do your work with enthusiasm. Work as if you were serving
the Lord, not as if you were serving only men and women.
EPHESIANS 6:7 NCV

My life is worth nothing unless I use it for doing the work
assigned me by the Lord Jesus.
ACTS 20:24 NLT

In all the work you are doing, work the best you can. Work as
if you were doing it for the Lord, not for people. Remember
that you will receive your reward from the Lord, which he
promised to his people. You are serving the Lord Christ.
COLOSSIANS 3:23-24 NCV

The plans of the diligent lead surely to abundance.
PROVERBS 21:5 NRSV

To enjoy your work . . . is indeed a gift from God.
ECCLESIASTES 5:19 TLB

ON THE JOB

God created the world out of nothing. He made stars and seashores, galaxies and grains of sand. He fashioned aspens, anteaters, and amniotic fluid. He breathed life into dust, crafting people who could freely choose whether they would love Him, hate Him, or ignore Him altogether. After His work was complete, God surveyed everything He'd done and declared it all good. Then, He celebrated what He had accomplished by taking some time off to relax and reflect.

As in everything, God provides a balanced example of how to live a full and fruitful life. Work is part of that life. Accomplishing tasks, creating, organizing, and nurturing all reflect the character of the One who created you in His image. That means your work matters to God—not just what you do, but the attitude and excellence with which you do it.

Whatever tasks you face today, consider them an assignment from God. Use the energy, creativity, and talents God has woven into your character to accomplish what needs to be done in a way that honors Him. Picture Him as your supervisor, encouraging you throughout the day with a "Good job!" here and a "Don't give up—you can do it!" there.

God wants to use you and your skills in amazing and unexpected ways. He wants you to know the joy and fulfillment that comes from a job well done. So remember, your work matters, even those little jobs that may seem insignificant at the time. Put your whole heart into what you do. Then, celebrate what you've accomplished with some time to relax and reflect in the presence of the One who is celebrating right along with you.

Worship

Ascribe to the Lord the glory of his name;
worship the Lord in holy splendor.

PSALM 29:2 NRSV

Oh come, let us worship and bow down;
Let us kneel before the LORD, our Maker.
For He is our God.

PSALM 95:6-7 NKJV

The LORD loves justice
and will not leave those who worship him.
He will always protect them.

PSALM 37:28 NCV

He put a new song in my mouth,
a song of praise to our God.

PSALM 40:3 NCV

God is honored by all who worship him.

PSALM 149:9 NCV

A LIFESTYLE OF PRAISE

Dancing to the rhythm of unabashed joy. Opening your home and your heart to someone in need. Living within your budget. Striving for excellence on the job. Sending a card to a downhearted friend. Taking part in Communion. Planting a rose garden. Writing your very own psalm. Sending money anonymously to a family that is struggling financially. Doing what God asks you to do. Watching a sunset. Working out at the gym. Thanking God for the food on your table. Coming to the aid of a stranger. Getting involved in a Bible study. Giving your husband a back rub. Singing with the church choir. Sharing with a friend about what God's doing in your life. Cheerfully giving money during your church's offering. Telling God just how wonderful He is. The list is endless.

When the music starts and the church choir or praise team stands up, everyone knows it's time to worship. But worship goes far beyond Sunday mornings, praise songs, and church walls. The ways you can worship God are as countless as the reasons there are to praise Him. Every minute of the day offers opportunities to show your devotion, adoration, respect, and gratitude to the God who holds you so close to His heart.

As moment by moment you become more aware that all of life is God's gift, how you live it becomes your thank-you note to Him. May today be a note God would love to read over and over again.

TOPICAL INDEX

Aging 10, 54, 98

Beauty 10, 12, 116, 180

Celebration 10, 14, 20, 74, 218, 220

Challenges 18, 90, 116, 138, 146, 162, 166

Change 20, 22, 60, 70, 92, 94, 106, 122, 140, 166, 174, 194

Character 12, 22, 62, 90, 116, 130, 156, 170, 212, 218

Church 26, 198, 220

Commitment 28, 62, 130, 134, 146, 154, 174, 186

Communication 30, 52, 74, 150, 170, 198

Compassion 34, 68, 76, 106, 108, 126, 170

Confidence 10, 36, 42, 66, 82, 100, 114, 162

Contentment 38, 58, 124, 188, 198

Courage 20, 42, 60, 66, 70, 98, 166, 196

Daily Walk 18, 26, 44, 50, 62, 66, 70, 74, 82, 84, 86, 90, 92, 94, 100, 114, 118, 122, 124, 130, 146, 154, 156, 158, 162, 170, 172, 174, 188, 194, 198, 202, 214, 218, 220

Doubt 46, 202

Emotions 18, 50, 66, 70, 98, 124, 126, 146, 162, 198, 202

Encouragement 52, 74, 82, 106, 116, 130, 146, 170, 198, 218, 220

Eternal Life 44, 54, 58, 60, 86, 142, 180, 198

Expectations 38, 58, 70, 76, 82, 84, 106, 110, 118, 130, 140, 196

Faith 18, 46, 60, 100, 106, 194, 206

Faithfulness 28, 62, 92, 170

Fear 20, 42, 66, 68, 70, 78, 110, 116

Forgiveness 68, 90, 94, 156, 172, 174, 178, 198, 210

Freedom 60, 66, 68, 70, 106, 116, 164, 198

Friendship 62, 74, 98, 132, 170

Generosity 34, 76

Gentleness 68, 78, 170

God's Faithfulness 60, 62, 66, 76, 82, 86, 94, 98, 100, 106, 110, 140, 156, 166, 188, 196

God's Love 14, 34, 36, 38, 68, 82, 84, 86, 92, 94, 98, 100, 106, 126, 134, 164, 166, 170, 178, 186, 198, 210, 212, 220

God's Presence 36, 66, 86, 100, 108, 122, 150, 162, 166, 188, 198

God's Will 42, 44, 58, 66, 70, 74, 90, 100, 108, 110, 130, 134, 174, 196, 206, 214, 218

God's Word 44, 46, 82, 90, 92, 100, 108, 150, 202, 210, 214

Grace 68, 94, 156, 178, 198

Grief 98, 126, 180

Guidance 44, 90, 100, 108, 174, 198

Guilt 70, 94, 102, 116, 156

Health 62, 106, 198

Holy Spirit 100, 108, 148, 182

Hope 60, 84, 98, 106, 108, 110, 126, 146, 180

Humility 78, 98, 114, 118

Identity 10, 12, 22, 62, 70, 114, 116, 118, 122, 130, 166, 178

Integrity 28, 62, 118, 124

Jesus Christ 60, 68, 94, 106, 114, 122, 126, 164, 170, 180, 186

Joy 70, 76, 92, 116, 124, 212, 218, 220

Love 78, 126, 154, 164, 170, 186, 190, 220

Ministry 62, 130, 170, 220

Nurturing 132

Obedience 42, 66, 100, 110, 134, 196, 214

Opposite Sex, The 100, 138, 156, 170

Patience 140, 194, 198, 206

Peace 70, 140, 142, 162, 198

Perseverance 28, 146, 196

Power 70, 108, 142, 148

Prayer 44, 98, 100, 106, 108, 148, 150, 162, 194, 198, 202

Priorities 28, 62, 74, 154, 174

Purity 94, 118, 156, 202

Purpose 20, 22, 28, 36, 42, 62, 66, 70, 84, 92, 110, 130, 142, 158, 166, 170, 174, 178, 204, 206, 212

Quietness and Solitude 86, 150, 162

Redemption 60, 68, 164

Rejection 166

Relationships 14, 26, 30, 62, 66, 74, 78, 98, 110, 132, 138, 146, 154, 170, 190, 194

Renewal 70, 98, 162, 172

Repentance 60, 94, 174

Restoration 68, 70, 94, 98, 126, 178

Resurrection 54, 126, 180

Righteousness 182

Sacrifice 164, 186

Seeking God 38, 86, 106, 122, 154, 172, 188

Sincerity 76, 190

Spiritual Growth 12, 22, 26, 46, 50, 70, 74, 82, 86, 92, 100, 118, 122, 130, 142, 148, 150, 162, 194, 214

Strength 36, 78, 98, 118, 148, 196, 198

Thankfulness 14, 150, 164, 186, 190, 198, 220

Thoughts 10, 18, 70, 146, 162, 202

Time 158, 204

Trials 20, 98, 146, 206, 212

Truth 70, 92, 116, 210

Vision 58, 84, 122, 130, 212

Wisdom 154, 204, 214

Work 130, 158, 218

Worship 190, 220

NOTES

1. Encarta World English Dictionary (reference tool on iMac), 4th definition of celebrate: "to praise something publicly or make it famous."

2. "Victorious Christians You Should Know" by Warren W. Wiersbe, 1984 Good News Broadcasting Assoc. (10th printing 1997 from Baker Book House) p. 100.

3. "Here Speeching American" by Kathryn Petras and Ross Petras, Villard Books Trade Paperback Original, 2004, p. 15, 17, 22.

4. "China: Eyewitness Travel Guides," edit. Hugh Thompson and Kathryn Lane. DK publishers, 2005, p. 31.

5. geyserstudy.org and Yellowstone-natl-park.com.

6. "Really Useful: the origins of everyday things" by Joel Levy, (Firefly Books Ltd, 2002, p. 135).

Unless otherwise marked, Scripture quotations are taken from the *Holy Bible, New International Version*®. NIV®.(North American Edition)®. Copyright © 1973, 1978, 1984 by International Bible Society. Used by permission of Zondervan Publishing House. All rights reserved.

Scripture quotations marked AMP are taken from *The Amplified Bible, Old Testament* copyright © 1965, 1987 by Zondervan Corporation, Grand Rapids, Michigan. *New Testament* copyright © 1958, 1987 by the Lockman Foundation, La Habra, California. Used by permission.

Scripture quotations marked KJV are taken from the *King James Version* of the Bible.

Scripture quotations marked MSG are taken from *The Message*. Copyright © by Eugene H. Peterson, 1993, 1994, 1995, 1996. Used by permission of NavPress Publishing Group.

Scripture quotations marked NASB are taken from the *New American Standard Bible*. Copyright © The Lockman Foundation 1960, 1962, 1963, 1968, 1971, 1972, 1973, 1975, 1977, 1995. Used by permission.

Scripture quotations marked NCV are taken from The Holy Bible, *New Century Version*®. Original work copyright © 1987, 1988, 1991 by Word Publishing, Dallas, Texas 75039. All rights reserved. Used by permission.

Scripture quotations marked NLT are taken from The Holy Bible, *New Living Translation*. Copyright © 1996. Used by permission of Tyndale House Publishers, Incorporated, Wheaton, Illinois 60189. All rights reserved.

Scripture quotations marked NRSV are taken from *The New Revised Standard Version* of the Bible. Copyright © 1989 by the Division of Christian Education of the National Council of the Churches of Christ in the United States of America. Used by permission. All rights reserved.

Scripture quotations marked RSV are taken from the *Revised Standard Version* of the Bible, New Testament section, First Edition, Copyright © 1946, New Testament, Second Edition, Copyright © 1971 by the Division of Christian Education of the National Council of the Churches of Christ in the United States of America. Used by permission.

Scripture quotations marked TLB are taken from *The Living Bible*. Copyright © 1971. Used by permission of Tyndale House Publishers, Incorporated, Wheaton, Illinois 60189. All rights reserved.

Scripture quotations marked NKJV are taken from The Holy Bible, *New King James Version*. Copyright © 1979, 1980, 1982, by Thomas Nelson, Inc. Used by permission.